VIRGIL AND SPENSER

BY

MERRITT Y. HUGHES

Tanta incohata res est, ut paene vitio mentis tantum opus ingressus mihi videar

AMS PRESS
NEW YORK

UNIVERSITY OF CALIFORNIA PUBLICATIONS IN ENGLISH
Volume 2, No. 3, pp. 263–418
Issued August 15, 1929

In this reprint the original pagination has been maintained
Reprinted from the edition of 1929, Berkeley
First AMS EDITION published 1971
Manufactured in the United States of America

International Standard Book Number: 0-404-07809-5

Library of Congress Number: 79-118629

AMS PRESS INC.
NEW YORK, N.Y. 10003

TO

A. Y. H.

CONTENTS

PART I

The Pastorals

I. VIRGIL'S *Eclogues* THROUGH A FRENCH LENS....... 265
II. THE PERSONAL ALLEGORY... 287
III. THE GHOST OF VIRGIL'S PASTORAL WORLD............ 295
IV. "E. K's" CRITICAL AUTHORITY................................. 302
V. CONCLUSION... 307
    Virgils Gnat. AN INTERCHAPTER............................ 309

PART II

The Epic and the Romance

I. "THE ENGLISH VIRGIL"... 317
II. EPIC VS. ROMANCE.. 322
III. VIRGIL'S WORLD IN SPENSER'S IMAGINATION........ 333
IV. THE COMMON CHARACTERS..................................... 348
V. MYTHOLOGY MADE PAGEANTRY AND ALLEGORY.. 365
VI. LANGUAGE AND IMAGE.. 382
VII. "THE ADMIRATION OF A PROFOUND PHILOSOPHER" 399
BIBLIOGRAPHY.. 407
INDEX.. 414

FOREWORD

This monograph was begun at Harvard University in 1920 as one of several essays on various classical influences upon the poetry of Spenser. One of those essays was published as "Spenser and the Greek Pastoral Triad" in April, 1923, in *Studies in Philology*. Its conclusion was that the Theocritean reminiscences in *The Shepheardes Calendar* were better to be understood as a result of Spenser's reading of the poetry of the *Pléiade* than as evidence that his imagination was haunted by direct recollections of the Sicilian poets. No such simple conclusion can be drawn from this essay. Spenser owed a very small and almost entirely indirect debt to Virgil's *Eclogues* but he must have loved the Hellenistic poems of Virgil's youth, the *Culex* and the *Ciris*, which the learned world may never quite agree to believe that Virgil really wrote. Unlike Ariosto, however, Spenser was certainly not an habitual reader of the *Aeneid* during his creative prime. His Virgilian echoes in *The Faerie Queene* seem like the memories of a time-hallowed but time-dimmed reverence for the *Aeneid*.

This little book will appeal to an audience which will inevitably be few and fit. The writer hopes that for Spenserians, although it repeats many things which Spenser's editors have said, it may throw some new light upon his poetry and upon his mind. For Virgilians it may have some interest as a kind of fragmentary sequel to Comparetti's great volumes on Virgil in the Middle Ages. To lovers of poetry in general, and of the poetry of the English Renaissance in particular, it may offer a few scattered flashes of imperfect penetration into the mystery of one poet's mind.

The Harvard thesis in which this essay has its roots was written under the direction of Professor John Livingston Lowes. To him the author owes hearty thanks. To the founders and directors of the John Simon Guggenheim Foundation he is indebted for the opportunity to supplement research done in Cambridge with the by-product of a year spent on another quest in the libraries of Rome and Florence.

MERRITT Y. HUGHES.

BERKELEY, CALIFORNIA
DECEMBER 7, 1928

PART I

THE PASTORALS

THE PASTORALS

I

VIRGIL'S *Eclogues* THROUGH A FRENCH LENS

Pastoral poetry in the sixteenth century was a hybrid between originality and imitation—between convention and revolt—but the difference between its parents was not so well understood then as it is now. Admiration of the classics was too absorbing a passion for men to create poetry confidently unless memories of their reading were the most powerful conscious ferment in their poetic experience. Originality was the handmaiden of Imitation, but in devious ways the handmaiden contrived to rival her lord. In the end, the passion for the Greek and Latin classics and for those newer classics inspired by them in Italy and in France was its own undoing. Among so many models individual taste must assert itself. The more catholic the passion for the classics became, the more eclectic it inevitably became. Fantastic eclecticism went hand in hand with an almost indiscriminate enthusiasm for the classics in the creative and critical work of the Renaissance, but nowhere more significantly than in the literary theories and in the pastoral poetry of the Frenchmen, Ronsard, Du Bellay, Baïf, and Daurat, who were the leaders of that *Brigade* or *Pléiade* which under Charles IX revolted brilliantly against "la populaire facilité, le terre-à-terre familier de la poésie frivole de l'école de Marot."—(Lanson, p. 277.)

The imitative theory found no better exemplars anywhere than Ronsard and his friends. They made it the first article of their creed that

> .... out of olde bokes, in good feith,
> Cometh al this newe science that men lere.

In *La Défense et l'Illustration de la Langue Françoise*[1] Du Bellay became the champion of the idea that there could be no authentic genius for poetry which was not nourished by a classical education and by enthusiastic classical tastes. In *La Défense*, however, as Brunetière remarked (*Evolution*, p. 42), "Les mots sont plus grands que les choses." By urging that a poet should convert the widest possible knowledge of the Greek, Latin, and Italian classics into "sang et nourriture" Du Bellay emancipated poetry from their definite control. His theory was a paradox, for it was seductively simple and yet inconsistent with itself. It came, as Brunetière has explained, when the time was ripe for it to be blindly accepted. Du Bellay declared that his contemporaries were the poetical heirs of the ancients, and pled that pastoral poetry should seek its inspiration and technique in the whole mass of bucolic literature inherited from Theocritus, as well as from his successors in Augustan Rome and in modern Italy and France. His idea was founded upon almost three centuries of cumulative tradition. Boccaccio's *Bucolicum Carmen* has more verbal reminiscences of Virgil than Virgil's *Eclogues* have of Theocritus. Sannazaro enlarged the pastoral tradition by widening its ramification into the past so as to include

---

[1] The importance of Du Bellay's argument in *La Défense* as the basis of many of the ideas in the text and commentary of Spenser's *Shepheardes Calendar* has been admirably studied by Renwick, *Edmund Spenser*, pp. 123–26, and by Fletcher in "Areopagus and Pléiade."

the *terza rima* of the *Divina Commedia* and the prose links of the *Vita Nuova*. The poets of the *Pléiade* rediscovered Virgil's Sicilian models and found new patterns in the *Greek Anthology* which they "imitated" in highly original ways. The French looked almost impartially upon their Greek, Latin, and Italian forerunners. "S'agit-il de fixer les modèles au futur chantre d'idylles? Les églogues de Sannazar figurent à côté des églogues de Théocrite et Virgile." (Chamard, *Joachim du Bellay*, pp. 62–63.)

When Spenser published *The Shepheardes Calendar* in 1579, he succeeded to the large liberty of "imitation" chartered by Du Bellay. We find him making his début with a series of twelve little idyls of which one ("October") is a free translation of Mantuan's fifth Eclogue, another ("November") a rendering of Marot's "Loyse de Savoy," still another ("December") a development from Marot's "Eglogue au Roy," while three others ("February," "May," and "September") contained beast fables which, to their creator, seemed to have a distinct Chaucerian flavor. The idyls in Spenser's "little boke" have no organic unity for readers of the twentieth century, but for his contemporaries they had the unity of a wonderful novelty sanctioned by their common root in the traditions of their *genre*. When it appeared, *The Shepheardes Calendar* seemed to mark the final step in a cumulative process of creative imitation which Virgil began when he filled his *Eclogues* with echoes of the pastorals of Theocritus. As the *Pléiade* had put Petrarch, Boccaccio, and Sannazaro on a footing of equality with Virgil and his Greek predecessors, so Spenser put Marot, whom Du Bellay despised as a barbarian, on a footing of equality with the Italians, and he exalted

Chaucer to the chief seat in his polyglot hierarchy. "E. K." summed up the situation in the first sentence of his letter commending to Gabriel Harvey "the patronage of the new poete":

> Uncouthe, unkiste, sayde the olde famous poete Chaucer: whom for his excellencie and wonderfull skil in making, his scholer Lidgate, a worthy scholler of so excellent a maister, calleth the loadestarre of our language: and whom our Colin Clout in his aeglogue calleth Tityrus the god of shepheardes—comparing hym to the worthines of the Roman Tityrus, Virgile. (*Cambridge Spenser*, p. 5.)

Mr. J. B. Fletcher has shown that the god of Spenser's critical idolatry when he was at work upon the *Calendar* was the Du Bellay of *La Défense et l'Illustration de la Langue Françoise*, and Mr. W. J. B. Pienaar ("Spenser and Jan van der Noot") has recently suggested that even before he left Cambridge Spenser was familiar with most of Ronsard's poetry. The whole story of the influence of the *Pléiade* upon Spenser can probably never be told. For us the important fact is that his French models seem to have liberated him from any superstitious respect that he may have had for Virgil's versification, while—as we shall find—they appear to have transmitted to him most of the Virgilian motifs and verbal reminiscences in *The Shepheardes Calendar*. In the patterns of their verse the poets of the *Pléiade* were the first to escape from the Virgilian tradition. The Latin hexameter had determined the rhythms of almost all the bucolics in Italian literature. The *terza rima* of Sannazaro's *Arcadia* was intended, like Dante's, to echo the *bello stilo*. Petrarch and Boccaccio had written their Latin eclogues in hexameters. The only pastoral poetry in

French which had attained any reputation before Baïf and Ronsard began to publish was by Clement Marot, and the rhythm of his eclogues beat as close an imitation as was possible in French pentameters of

The stateliest measure ever moulded by the lips of man.

Ronsard, however, wrote in octosyllabic couplets as well as in pentameters, and Baïf varied his meters with almost as many lyric measures as Spenser crowded into the *Calendar*. Like Spenser also, the French admitted every kind of subject and wrote "églogues terrestres et marines, églogues baptismales, églogues matrimoniales, églogues funèbres. Il y a même des églogues sans bergers: pour Marie de Romieu la bucolique n'est qu'une élégie amoureuse." (Augé-Chiquet, *Baïf*, pp. 252-53.)

It was Baïf who really created French pastoral poetry by letting his enthusiasm for eclectic imitation carry him as far as it would. To his later contemporaries he seemed to have been the inventor of the *genre*. Vauquelin hailed him as a pioneer.

> Baïf et Tahureau, tous les mêmes années,
> Avions par les forests ses Muses pourmenées:
> Belleau, qui vient après, nostre langage estant
> Plus abondant et douce, la nature imitant
> Egalla tous Bergers.
> —*Art poetique*, p. 89.

Baïf's example and Du Bellay's critical attack upon Marot's reputation outlawed facile imitation of Virgil. By increasing the range of the pastoral, as Vauquelin's lines suggest, they carried it a long stage on the road to independence. Thenceforth it could never again be content to repeat a Virgilian melody; it must try to harmonize elaborate centos of reminiscence from the most diverse sources, or else seek to adapt Greek music to a French instrument. Of the nineteen eclogues by Baïf, seven were composite, eleven were translated, and of these a majority had Greek originals. "Théocrite est le modèle de prédilection," observes Baïf's biographer (Augé-Chiquet, *Baïf*, p. 253). "Baïf a traduit en entier cinq de ses idylles." Baïf's preference for Theocritus was characteristic. The gaiety of the Greek idyls was closer to the spirit of the French Renaissance than was the prevailing tone of Virgil's pastorals. Nothing in Virgil's *Eclogues* was so readily assimilable as were idyls such as Theocritus' "Cyclops," which became Baïf's eighth Eclogue. Virgil's sympathy with rural life and rural scenery escaped Baïf, but he readily appropriated the pleasure in a festive picnic like that described by Theocritus in the "Harvesters," to which he gave a French dress in his fourteenth Eclogue.

Baïf's indebtedness to Virgil has been summarized in detail by M. Augé-Chiquet, whose analysis is worth quoting for comparison with the extent and kind of indebtedness to Virgil displayed by *The Shepeardes Calendar*:

La quinzième églogue est traduite en entier du poème des *Dirae*, longtemps attribué à Virgile. Plusieurs sont composées par contamination. Virgile a donné l'idée première et les parties les plus importantes de "Brinon"; Sannazar a fourni pour ce poème une douzaine de vers; le reste est de Baïf. La quatrième, "Marmot," offrit un mélange de Virgile et de Théocrite; dans les églogues cinquième et seizième ("Les Sorcières," "La Sorcière") c'est le plus bizarre assemblage des inventions de Théocrite, de Virgile, et de Sannazar, auxquelles Baïf vient ajouter les siennes propres. Enfin, la neuvième est une véritable marqueterie. On y retrouve des fragments de deux églogues de Virgile, une idylle de Bion, et deux métamorphoses d'Ovide; encore toutes les parties de ce poème n'ont-elles pu être identifiées. Labeur d'ouvrier appliqué, non d'artiste. Une seule préoccupation obsède l'esprit de Baïf; il veut enrichir son sujet, le charger d'ornements empruntés, accumuler les episodes, fussent-ils disparates. (*Baïf*, pp. 253-54.)

In *The Shepeardes Calendar* English, French, and Italian poets overshadowed their classical predecessors[2] even more completely than they did for Baïf. Modern critics have agreed with "E. K." in attributing a classical foundation to only one of Spenser's eclogues as a whole. That poem is "August," which (as "E. K." remarked in his Argument) sets "forth a delectable controversie, made in imitation of that in Theocritus, whereunto Virgile also fashioned his third and seventh Aeglogue." Before we accept the tradition that Spenser wrote his "August" with recollections of Theocritus and Virgil fermenting in his mind, we shall have to examine the eclogue in very close detail. Four distinct motifs in "August" interest us: the challenge to the singing match, the pledges of the contestants, the election of the judge, and his diplomatic decision.

[2] Marot is the strongest constituting influence in the *Calendar*, for "November" and "December" are based almost entirely upon translation from him. Mantuan, with "October" to his credit almost literally, stands next. But the balance swings sharply in Chaucer's favor if we take account of *Mother Hubberds Tale*, of *Daphnaida*, and of the fables in "February," "July," and "September." *Vide* Cory, *Edmund Spenser*, p. 197, and Nadal, "Spenser's *Muiopotmos* in relation to Chaucer's *Sir Thopas*," and "Spenser's *Daphnaida* and Chaucer's *Book of the Duchess*."

THE CHALLENGE

M. Augé-Chiquet, in the summary just quoted, points out that Baïf actually did in his fourth Eclogue what "E. K." asserts that Spenser did in "August." He made a mélange of Virgil and Theocritus. The Theocritean motif of the singing contest, which Virgil in his third Eclogue made into a conventionalized 'flyting,' was the most temptingly imitable feature in the gamut of themes found in Greek and Latin pastoral poetry. There would be little significance for us in Baïf's anticipation of Spenser's use of this "Virgilian" machinery in "August" if Ronsard[3] and Sir Philip Sidney[3] also had not used it in pastorals for which Spenser probably had a lively admiration. Sidney, Baïf, and Ronsard all made Virgil's song contest their general pattern, but for them all the dramatic device served as a melody which each man harmonized in accordance with his own whim. Both Baïf and Sidney combined with it some reminiscences of Theocritus and a debt to Sannazaro, out of deference to whom Sidney threw the amoebaean part of his poem into *terza rima*. There is a striking agreement between the features of Virgil's third Eclogue as they were appropriated respectively by Baïf in "Marmot" and by Sidney in "Nico and Dorus." Sidney took less than Baïf from Virgil, but he took nothing for the theft of which he did not have the Frenchman's example. There is no question, probably, of a parody of Baïf, for Sidney's burlesque 'flyting' mocked a fashion rather than an individual. To the carnival

---

[3] *Vide* Storer, *Virgil and Ronsard*, p. 88, and Grosart's notes and text of "Nico and Dorus" in his *Complete Poems of Sir Philip Sydney*, 11:187–97.

gaiety of such pastorals as "Marmot," however, "Nico and Dorus" owed its contrast with the sententious playfulness of Virgil's amoebaeans.

The openings of Sidney's and of Baïf's poems are both plainly based upon Virgil:

MENALCAS. Dic mihi, Damoetas, cuium pecus ? an Meliboei ?
DAMOETAS. Non, verum Aegonis; nuper mihi tradidit Aegon.
MENALCAS. Infelix o semper, ovis, pecus! ipse Naearam
　　　　　　Dum fovet, ac, ne me sibi praeferat illa, veretur,
　　　　　　Hic alienus ovis custos bis mulget in hora,
　　　　　　Et sucus pecori et lac subducitur agnis.

Baïf translated this superliterally, making all the nuances of Virgil's irony explicit.

IAQUIN. Dy moy, Marmot, qui est le pauvre et simple maistre
　　　　Qui t'a ainsi donné tous ses troupeaux a paistre,
　　　　Et comment si soudain d'un ord vilain porchier
　　　　Que tu estois antan, tu t'as fait un vachier ?
MARMOT. De quoy te soucis tu ? Tu as bien peu que faire,
　　　　Iaquin, de t'enquerir ainsi de mon affaire.
IAQUIN. O malheureux le maistre ! o bestail malheureux !
　　　　Cependant que Marmot de Margot amoureux !
　　　　Qui a peur qu'en amour Berlem ne le devance,
　　　　A fin d'entretenir de ses dons sa bobance,
　　　　Pour vendre le laitage a toute heure le trait,
　　　　Aux vaches & aux veaux derobent tout le lait.
　　　　　　　　　　—*Oeuvres*, III: 21.

Sidney's opening lines are not distinctly imitated from Virgil, but they are interesting because they suggest Spenser's beginning to "September," which is the eclogue following that under discussion. Sidney wrote:

Nico. And are you there, old Pas ! In troth, I ever thought
   Among us all we should find something of nought.
Pas. And I am here the same, so mote I thrive and thee,
   Despairde in all this flocke to find a knave but thee.

In Spenser's "August," though Virgil's opening situation is used, there is no trace of the traditional curtain-raiser of jibes. Like all its vague prototypes, "August" is a play within a play, but the preliminary dialogue is a lovelorn swain's confession in which the traditional hit about the hungry flocks of lovers is given a humorless and sentimental turn. The song-contest is proposed as an antidote for the hapless lover's woe.

Willye. Perdie and wellawaye ! ill may they thrive:
   Never knew I lovers sheepe in good plight.
   But and if in rymes with me thou dare strive,
   Such fond fantsies shall soone be put to flight.
            —Lines 19–22.

Perigot accepts the challenge and the two shepherds appoint Cuddie their umpire. Spenser, unlike Baïf and Sidney, adds an un-Virgilian feature in a final song by the judge. The contest itself, which is the *raison d'être* of Virgil's Eclogue, is subordinated by Baïf and burlesqued by Sidney, who used "Nico and Dorus" for comic relief in the *Arcadia*. In the light of the irresponsible imitation of Virgil's third Eclogue by Sidney and by Baïf we can afford to smile a little at Professor Herford's disappointment that Spenser's "Willy and Perigot carry on their contest, not in the polished and sonorous couplets of Theocritus and Virgil, but with hurried snatches of phrase in the homely meter of the ballads which every village Autolycus dispensed to the Mopsas of the countryside." (*Cal-*

endar, ed. Herford, p. xliii.) Professor Herford makes no allowance for the reaction of Spenser and his contemporaries against pastoral poetry which had been written out of a too superficial admiration for the Virgilian sonority. When Sidney wrote his poetic interlude in the *Arcadia* he gave his readers an amusing burlesque of the conventional amoebaeans in pedestrian pentameters parodying Virgil's hexameters. We shall not be far from the truth if we regard Spenser's roundelay in "August" as having been written in a spirit of experiment nearly related to Sidney's satirical purpose.

Sidney and Baïf both imitated the brags which Virgil's rustics exchange. Baïf's lines are a literal translation:

MARMOT. Voire da: mais pourquoy ne m'eust-il pas rendue,
Puis qu'il avoit gagé, la gajure perdue ?
Cet agnelet (a fin que tu le saches bien)
Qu'a chanter je gagnay, de bon gain estoit mien.
IAQUIN. A chanter, toy Marmot ? mais as-tu de ta vie
A toy pour un jouer, aucune chalemie ?
Que tu gagnas Toinet ? comment le-gagnas-tu ?
Tu ne souflas jamais que dedans un festu.
—Lines 18–25.

The French is a perfect rendering of the Latin:

DAMOETAS. An mihi cantando victus non rederret ille,
Quem mea carminibus meruisset fistula caprum ?
Si nescis, meus ille caper fuit; et mihi Damon
Ipse fatebatur; sed reddere posse negabat.
MENALCAS. Cantando tu illum ? aut umquam tibi fistula cera
Iuncta fuit ? non tu in triviis, indocte, solebas
Stridenti miserum stipula disperdere carmen ?
—Lines 21–27.

Sidney paraphrased Virgil by making his peasants mouth the classical jibes in speech of more than Wordsworthian simplicity.

PAS. My voice the lambe did winne, Menalcas was our judge;
　　Of singing match was made, whence he with shame did trudge.
NICO. Could'st thou make Lalus flie ? So nightingales avoid
　　When with a kawing crowe their musick is annoide.
PAS. Nay, like to nightingales the other birds give care;
　　My pipe and song made him both pipe and song forsweare.
NICO. I think it will; such voice would make one musicke hate;
　　But if I had beene there th'hadst met another mate.
PAS. Another sure as is a gander from a goose;
　　But still, when thou dost sing, methinks a colt is loose.
NICO. Well aimed, by my hat; for as thou sang'st last day,
　　The neighbors all did crie, Alas, what asse did bray ?
　　　　　　—Lines 16–26.

Spenser compressed the motif of the exchange of insults into two verses:

PERIGOT. That shall I doe, though mochell worse I fared:
　　Never shall be sayde that Perigot was dared.
　　　　　　—Lines 23–24.

At the conclusion of the challenges Baïf introduced a feature which is not found in Virgil's third or seventh Eclogues. Sidney and Spenser both followed him in this innovation. The coincidence may be an accident, but it encourages the belief that both English poets were familiar with Baïf's poem. His innovation consists in twenty original lines of trifling about Marmot's mistress in which the substance of Spenser's roundelay is suggested. As a whole, of course, the attitude toward love in "August"—as in the *Calendar* generally—contrasts by its Puritanism with that in Baïf's Eclogue. This leads to an echo of Virgil's warning about "the tangles of Neaera's hair." Perigot's confession of youthful disillusion in the lines,

> Love hath misled both my younglings and mee:
> I pyne for payne, and they my payne to see.
> —Lines 17–18.

directly recalls Menalcas' verse,

> Infelix o semper, ovis, pecus ! ipse Neaeram
> Dum fovet.

THE PLEDGES

Before Spenser's shepherds begin their singing match Willye plights a pledge:

> A mazer ywrought of the maple warre:
> Wherein is enchased many a fayre sight
> Of beres and tygres, that maken fiers warre;
> And over them spred a goodly wild vine,
> Entrailed with a wanton yvie-twine.
>
> Thereby is a lambe in the wolves jawes:
> But see, how fast renneth the shepheard swayne,
> To save the innocent from the beastes pawes;
> And here with his shepehooke hath him slayne.
> Tell me, such a cup hast thou ever sene ?
> —Lines 26–35.

Perigot rejoins:

> Thereto will I pawne yonder spotted lambe;
> Of all my flocke there nis sike another;
> For I brought him up without the dambe.
> —Lines 37–39.

"A mazer" "E. K." glossed with the remark that, "So also did Theocritus and Virgile feigne pledges of their strife." He might have mentioned also Ronsard and Baïf and we can add to his list Sidney, who burlesqued the motif:

Nico. I will lay a wager hereunto,
That profit may ensue to him that best can do.
I have, and long shall have, a white great nimble cat,
A king upon a mouse, a strong foe to the rat;
Fine eares, long taile he hath, with lion's curbed clawe,
Which oft he lifteth up and stayes his lifted pawe,
Deepe musing to himselfe, which after-mewing shewes,
Till, with the lickt beard, his eye of fire espie his foes.

Pas. I have a better match,
A prettie curre it is, his name i-wis is Catch;
No eare or taile he hath, least they should him disgrace.
A ruddie haire his cote, with fine long spectled face;
He never musing standes, but with himselfe will play,
Leaping at every flie, and angrie with a flee;
He eft would kill a mouse, but he disdaines to fight,
And makes our home good sport with dauncing bolt upright.
—Lines 29–35, 39–46.

"E. K." is accurate in attributing this motif of the pledges to both Theocritus and Virgil (Theocritus, Idyl V, vv. 22–30, and Virgil, Eclogue III, vv. 29–43), but the details of their treatments of it do not resemble any of the traits in Spenser's passage. With Virgil the motif took the following form:

Damoetas. Vis ergo, inter nos, quid possit uterque vicissim.
Experiamur ? ego hanc vitulam—ne forte recuses,
Bis venit ad mulctram, binos alit ubere fetus—
Depono; tu dic, mecum quo pignore certes.

MENALCAS. De grege non ausim quicquam deponere tecum:
Est mihi namque domi pater, est injusta noverca:
Bisque die numerant ambo pecus, alter et haedos.[4]
Verum, id quod multo tute ipse fatebere maius,
Insanire libet quoniam tibi, pocula ponam
Fagina, caelatum divini opus Alcimedontis:
Lenta quibus torno facili superaddita vitis
Diffusos haedera vestit pallente corymbos.
In medio duo signa, Conon, et—quis fuit alter—
Descripsit radio totum qui gentibus orbem,
Tempora quae messor, quae curvus arator
haberet.
Necdum illis labra admovi, sed condita servo.

DAMOETAS. Et nobis idem Alcimedon duo pocula fecit,
Et molli circum est ansas amplexus acantho,
Orpheaque in medio posuit silvasque sequentis.
Necdum illis labra admovi, sed condita servo.
Si ad vitulam spectas, nihil est, quod pocula
laudes.
—Lines 28–48.

---

[4] This stroke about the *injusta noverca* was a favorite touch with all writers of pastoral in the Renaissance. It left no trace where we would expect it, in "August," but in "March" Spenser made use of it in the lines

WILLYE. For als at home I have a syre,
A stepdame eke, as whott as fyre,
That dewly adayes counts mine.
—Lines 40–42.

Reissert indicated occurrences of this touch in Mantuan and in Boccaccio, and to his parallels we may add one from Baïf, Eclogue IV, where the challenger uses it:

... tu n'oserois gager rien de troupeau,
Songe que tu me mettras.

Compare Mantuan, VII: 59:

Durus et imitis pater atque superba noverca.

And Boccaccio, XIII: 673–74:

Deponam vitulam, qua non est pinguior ulla
Armentis, etiam. si clamitet inde noverca.

It has been urged[5] that Spenser's representation of two stages of action in the glyptic ornamentation of his cup makes it likely that he was imitating Theocritus rather than Virgil. Because Virgil dismisses the second element in his composite picture with the broken phrase, "Quis fuit alter?" while Theocritus crowded into his picture the action of a tiny drama in two scenes, it has been gravely concluded that the Greek eclogue was Spenser's "source." Yet Sannazaro's *Arcadia*, Prosa Terza, repeats the motif with the Theocritean double action and in the French pastorals it is regularly found with the composite picture. Baïf in his fourth Eclogue, "Marmot," has a French shepherd boy make a cup decorated with an intaglio ornament his stake in a singing-match.

> Ie va mettre un vaisseau,
> Un beau vaisseau de buys, que chèrement ie garde,
> De l'oeuvre de Francin: aucun ne le regarde
> Qui, pamant de le voir si proprement ouvré,
> Ne s'enquiere de moy dou ie l'ay recouvré.
>   Sous le ventre Silen le creux du vase porte
> Monté dessus son asne & ce roidist de forte
> Qu'en voit son col nouveux s'enfler sous le fardeau,
> Comme si'il ahanoit a porter le vaisseau.
> Tout alentour de lui une vigne rampante
> Traine a mont du vaisseau mainte grappe pendante:
> Maints amoureux aislez & derriere & devant
> De sagettes & d'arcs touchent l'asne en avant,
> Et maints autres tous nus sans arcs & sans sagettes,
> Grimpans a mont les cep, de tranchantes serpettes,
> Coupent les raisins meurs en des petits cofins;
> D'autres foulent en bas en des cuves les vins.

---

[5] By Reissert in his note on "August," l. 34, and by Kerlin, in *Theocritus in English Literature*, pp. 24–25.

> A l'environ du pied maint sautelant Satyre,
> Les Tygres & Lyons de longues resnes tire,
> Qui conduisent Bacchus de pampre couronné,
> Assis dessous un char d'ierre environné.
> Ie mettray ce vaisseau fait de telle bossure,
> Tout neuf comme ie l'ay: car pour vray ie t'assure
> Qu'a ma bouche jamais nul ne l'a vu toucher,
> Mais ie te le mettray, combien qu'il me soit cher.
> —*Le Pléiade française*, III: 24-25.

In the pastorals of Ronsard descriptions of glyptic ornaments occur, in all, four times. Once the motif is developed as a close paraphrase of Theocritus' vignette of the boy weaving traps for grasshoppers and quite unconscious that a fox in the background is spoiling the vines:

> Aux pieds de ceste nymphe est un garçon qui semble
> Cueillir des brins de jonc et les lier ensemble
> De long et de travers courbé sur le genou.
> Il les presse du pouce et les serre d'un noud,
> Puis il fait entre-deux des fenestres égales,
> Façonnant une cage a mettre des Cigales.
>
> Loin derrière son dos est gisante à l'escart
> Sa panetiere enflée, en laquelle un Renard
> Met le nez finement, et d'une ruze estrange
> Trouve le desjeuner du garcon et le mange,
> Dont l'enfant s'apperçoit sans estre courroucé,
> Tant il est ententif a l'oeuvre commencé.
>
> Si mettray-ie pourtant une telle houlette
> Que j'estime en valeur autant qu'une musette.
> —Laumonier's edition, III: 365.

Dramatic action is the essence of all Ronsard's descriptions of carved cups. They are always plays within plays, tiny *idyllia* within idyls. Ronsard must have regarded them as one of the final technical refinements of the pastoral and as a delicate application of the (falsely interpreted) Horatian principle, *Ut picutra poesis*. None of Ronsard's intaglios has the simple gravity of Virgil's picture of Conon, who

> Descripsit radio totum qui gentibus orbem,
> Tempora quae messor, quae curvus arator haberet.

At one stroke in these verses Virgil traced the outlines of the *Georgics*. Ronsard's descriptions of glyptic ornaments, like the following from his fifth eclogue, are much more likely to anticipate the over-civilized detachment of piscatory pastorals than they are to reflect a practical interest in "a shepherd's life."

> Un Pescheur est assis au bord du Gobelet,
> Qui courbé fait semblant de ietter un filet
> Dans la mer pour pescher, puis de toute sa force
> Et de mains & de nerfs & de veines s'efforce
> De le tirer sur l'eau: ses muscles grands & gros
> S'enflent depuis son chef iusqu'au bas de son dos:
> Tout le front luy degoutte, & bien qu'il soit vieil homme,
> Le labeur toutefois ses membres ne consomme.
> —Laumonier's edition, III: 440.

Here there is nothing Virgilian. The picture is taken from the first idyl of Theocritus but, in spite of his partly literal rendering of the Greek, Ronsard was not attracted by the realistic drawing of a sea-beaten old fisherman. His description faintly and sentimentally adumbrates the *Ode to a Grecian Urn*.

> Thou, silent form, dost tease us out of thought
> As doth Eternity: Cold Pastoral.

Spenser, when he "enchased many a fayre sight of beres and tygres" on his cup, may have remembered that he had Theocritean and Virgilian warrant for doing so but we can hardly doubt he learned the magic of such scene-painting from Ronsard.

THE JUDGE

Two more Virgilian motifs remain to be considered in "August"; the election of the judge in the song-contest and his dubious award. Both seem to owe their form and perhaps their existence itself to French rather than to Latin influence. Spenser wrote:

WILLYE. But who shall judge the wager wonne or lost?
PERIGOT. That shall yonder heardgrome, and none other,
    Which over the pousse hetherward doth post.
                  —Lines 44–46.

Cuddie's casual approach "over the pousse" is like Palaemon's arrival at the "critical moment" in Virgil's third Eclogue.

MENALCAS. Nunquam hodie effugies; veniam, quocumque
        vocaris.
    Audiat haec tantum—vel qui venit, ecce, Palae-
        mon.
    Efficiam posthac ne quemquam voce lacessas.
DAMOETAS. Quin age, si quid habes, in me mora non erit ulla,
    Nec quemquam fugio: tantum, vicine Palaemon,
    Sensibus haec imis, res est non parva, reponas.
PALAEMON. Dicite, quandoquidem in molli consedimus herba.
                  —Lines 49–55.

The election of the judge in Baïf's "Marmot" and in Sidney's "Nico and Dorus," however, corresponds in both cases more closely with Virgil's scene than does Spenser's. Ronsard also reproduced this motif of the invitation of a chance comer to sit down in the shade with the contestants as their judge (in his fourth Eclogue, Laumonier's edition, III, 428). Again in this case, the conclusion that Spenser's "auctoritie" was Gallic rather than Latin seems justified.

THE AWARD

The final Virgilian convention in "August" is the drawn decision made by Cuddie.

CUDDIE. Sicker, sike a roundle never heard I none.
   Little lacketh Perigot of the best,
   And Willye is not greatly overgone,
   So weren his undersongs well addrest.
WILLYE. Herdgrome, I fear me thou have a squint eye;
   Areede uprightly, who has the victorye?
CUDDIE. Fayth of my soule, I deeme ech have gayned.
   Forthy let the lambe be Willye his owne;
   And for Perigot so well hath hym payned,
   To him be the wroughten mazer alone.
                              —Lines 125–134.

Baïf in "Marmot" and Sidney in "Nico and Dorus" come to abrupt endings parodying or burlesquing Virgil. Sidney's judge, Dicus, exclaims:

   Enough, enough, so ill hath done the best,
   That since the having them to neither's due,
   Let cat and dog fight which shall have both you.[6]

---

[6] Sidney ends his pastoral by crowning his crime of *lèse majesté* against Virgil with a grotesque imitation of his closing riddles:
   DAMOETAS. Dic, quibus in terris—et eris mihi magnus Apollo—
      Tris pateat caeli spatium non amplius ulnas.
   MENALCAS. Dic, quibus in terris inscripti nomine regum
      Nascantur flores, et Phyllida solus habeto.
Sidney wrote:
   NICO. Tell me (and be my Pan) the monster's name
      That has foure legs, and with two only goes;
      That has foure eyes, and onely two can frame.
   PAS. Tell me (and Phoebus be) what monster growes
      Sith so strange lives that bodie cannot rest
      In ease, untill that bodie life foregoes.

Ronsard ends the formal singing contest of his first Eclogue with an embroidery upon the same convention. The second "Berger voyageur" says:

> L'un sur l'autre n'aura le pris victorieux,
> Estans également les chers mignons des Dieux.
> Apollon & Palés & Pan vous favorisent,
> Et tous à qui mieux vous honorent & prisent:
>
> Et pource abandonnez vos prix & vos discords,
> Et venez escouter les merveilleux accords
> De deux pères Bergers, qui dessous une roche
> Vont dire une chanson dont Tityre n'approche.
> —Laumonier's edition, III: 386.

In conclusion, then, we may say that, read in the perspective of the French renaissance, Spenser's "August" as a whole seems very remotely Virgilian. Its echoes of Virgil's third and seventh Eclogues all appear to have been transmitted to it through the pastoral poetry of the *Pléiade*. The frequent and often brilliant treatment by Ronsard, Baïf, and Du Bellay of the four "Virgilian" motifs which have just been studied, must have fired Spenser's enthusiasm. Had he known them only as they are found in Latin and Greek literature, it is very doubtful whether any of them would have appeared in his pastorals. Every feature in *August* was passing or had passed into a dying tradition when Spenser published the *Calendar* in 1579. Its conventions were ripe for parody when Sidney was writing the *Arcadia*, and in 1597 Hall, in the "Defiance to Envy" which he prefixed to his *Satires*, stamped them all as having reached the point of impotent petrifaction.

Or list us make two striving shepherds sing,
With costly wagers for the victory,
Under Menalcas judge; while one doth bring
A carven bowl well wrought of beechen tree,
    Praising it by the story or the frame,
    Or want of use, or skilful maker's name.

Another layeth a well marked lamb,
Or spotted kid, or some more forward steer,
And from the pail doth praise their fertile dam;
So do they strive in doubt, in hope, in fear,
    Awaiting for their trusty umpire's doom,
    Faulted as false by him that's overcome.
               —Singer's edition, p. ciii.

II

THE PERSONAL ALLEGORY
SPENSER HIMSELF

In Spenser's introduction of himself in the allegory of *The Shepheardes Calendar* under the name of Colin Clout "E. K." characteristically traced an act of homage to Virgil's authority. He glossed the first appearance of the name in January ingeniously as follows:

Colin Clout is a name not greatly used, and yet have I sene a poesie of Maister Skeltons under that title. But indeed the word Colin is Frenche, and used of the French poete Marot (if he be worthy the name of a poete) in a certein aeglogue. Under which name this poete [i.e., Spenser] secretly shadoweth himself, as sometime did Virgil under the name Tityrus, thinking it much fitter then such Latine names, for the great unlikelyhoode of the language.

"E. K." does not seem to have been aware that Virgil's commentators from the earliest times have observed that his rôle in the allegory of his Eclogues was indicated under a protean variety of names, and he cannot be blamed for failing to foresee the doubts which modern scholarship has raised about the identification of the Tityrus of the Eclogues with Virgil.[7] Ronsard

---

[7] Niccola Terzaghi in *L'Allegoria nelle Egloghe di Virgilio*, p. 24, points out that Vives took Menalcas in the third Eclogue as personifying Virgil's detractors and Damoetas as representing Virgil himself. On pp. 26-30 he summarizes the opinions of the Virgilian commentators from Servius down and indicates general disagreement among them. DeWitt in *Virgil's Autobiographia Literaria*, p. 159, argues that all of Virgil's *Eclogues* were written after Augustus' return from Greece in 41 B.C., and that they therefore had nothing to do with Virgil's personal fortunes. Their theme, he suggests, is general, not personal at all. Virgil is pleading for tranquillity for Italy and Tityrus is a name which symbolized for his readers the average, middle-aged Italian peasant whom the civil wars had ruined. On p. 129, in discussing the shifting identity of Tityrus and of other names in the *Eclogues*, DeWitt remarks that "the novelty of Virgil's *facetiae* appears to consist in the deliberate planning of ambiguous allusions." Frank, in *Virgil, a Biography*, p. 129, is in substantial agreement with DeWitt. Compare Prescott's splendid discussion in *Virgil's Art*, pp. 95-117.

appeared under changed names in his third and fourth Eclogues;[8] Baïf assumed various rôles in his pastorals; and Boccaccio in the early poems of the *Bucolicum Carmen* identified himself otherwise than by the name of Silvius, which he took in the eclogue most familiar to English readers, the fourteenth, "Olympia." All of these continental poets were therefore nearer to Virgil's practice in this matter (unless, as Prescott believes, Virgil obtrudes little or no personal allegory in the Eclogues) than was Spenser, who, with only one exception, seems to have used the name Colin Clout for himself throughout all his pastorals from *The Shepheardes Calendar* to *Colin Clouts come home again*. In "October" he took the name of Cuddie, but in "January," "April," "June," and "December," in *Daphnaida*, and in the Pastorella incident in *The Faerie Queene* he is Colin Clout. The reflections of his experience by Colin—to use his own language to Sir Walter Raleigh in his dedication of *Colin Clouts come home again*,—"agree," often unpoetically, "with the truth in circumstance and matter." For us the important thing to notice is that Spenser's shadowing of himself in his pastoral allegories contrasts with Virgil's by being in the main consistent, sometimes querulous, and always a little emphatic.

GABRIEL HARVEY

The personal allegory in Virgil's Eclogues is a series of fantasies founded upon his memories of several cordial friendships. Nowhere in the *Calendar* is there anything corresponding to the gracious intimacies recorded in Virgil's "Pollio," "Varus," and

---

[8] *Vide* the notes of Blanchemain in his edition of Ronsard's *Oeuvres*, IV: 54 and 82.

"Gallus." M. Legouis remarks that never in Spenser's verse or prose do we find "the thrilling accents of Montaigne commemorating his love for La Boetie or of Shakespeare sacrificing to the young friend of the *Sonnets* his soul, his pride and his genius." (*Spenser*, p. 14.) There is only one salient record of a friendship in the *Calendar* and in that there is really nothing whatever which resembles Virgil's tributes to his intimates, but it happens to contain a very curious use of a line from Virgil's second Eclogue, "Alexis," which won wide currency in the Renaissance. In "January," "April," "June," and "December," Gabriel Harvey, Spenser's teacher and friend at Cambridge, has a very doubtful rôle as Hobbinol. Spenser's attitude seems sentimentally patronizing. He looks back upon his intimacy with Harvey as a loyalty surviving from undergraduate adolescence. Colin confesses in "January" that Rosalind—who may be the Lancashire beauty imagined by Grosart, but who is probably the symbol of an *éducation sentimentale* in which, as Harvey himself suggested in his correspondence with his young friend, one "Rosalindula" succeeded another—has estranged him from his old friend.

COLIN. It is not Hobbinol wherefore I plaine,
Albee my love he seeke with dayly suit;
His clownish gifts and curtsies I disdaine,
His kiddes, his cracknelles and his early fruit.
Ah, foolish Hobbinol! thy gifts bene vayne;
Colin them gives to Rosalind againe.
—Lines 55–60.

In "April" Hobbinol tells his side of the story to Thenot.

HOBBINOL. Colin thou kenst, the Southerne shepheardes
               boye;
           Him Love hath wounded with a deadly darte:
           Whilome on him was all my care and joye,
           Forcing with gyfts to winne his wanton heart.
           But now from me hys madding mynd is starte,
           And woes the widowes daughter of the glenne:
           So nowe fayre Rosalind hath bredde hys smart,
           So now his frend is chaunged for a frenne.
                       —Lines 21–28.

"E. K." did not fail to point out the resemblance here to Virgil's "Alexis" and to compare Hobbinol's rejected gifts in "January" to those of Corydon.

Rusticus es, Corydon; nec munera curat Alexis.
                       —Line 56.

And then, seemingly with an obscure recollection of the evil tradition which from the earliest times has tainted Virgil's character,[9] he indulged in a gloss of curious pruriency:

In thys place seemeth to be some savour of disorderly love, which the learned call *paederastice*: but it is gathered beside his meaning. For who that hath red Plato his dialogue called *Alcybiades*, Xenophon, and Maximus Tyrius, of Socrates opinions, may easily perceive that such love is muche to be allowed and liked of, specially so meant as

[9] Terzaghi, *L'Allegoria*, pp. 34–46, summarizes the history of ancient and medieval commentary upon the second Eclogue which established the tradition that Virgil was homosexual. The tradition goes back to a passage in Donatus' *Life of Virgil* which I quote from Phaer's rendering of it in his preface to his translation of the *Aeneid* in the (unpaged) edition of 1584.

"Some report that he [Virgil] was prone to the detestable sinne with boyes. But the better sort suppose rather that he loved them as Socrates Alcibiades, and Plato also. Above the rest he loved most Cebetes, and Alexander, who in the second Eclogue of his *Bucolikes* he termeth Alexis."

Renwick in *Spenser*, p. 135, suggests that Spenser derived his "exposition of the Graces in the Sixth Book of *The Faerie Queene* from Servius' *Commentary*. The *Commentary* was certainly responsible for some of the biographical ideas about Virgil which were entertained by Spenser and his annotator.

Socrates used it: who sayth, that in deede he loved Alcybiades extremely, yet not Alcybiades person, but hys soule, which is Alcybiades owne selfe. And so is *paederastice* muche to be praeferred before *gynerastice*, that is, the love whiche enflameth with lust toward womankind.

The literature of the Renaissance was full of stories about both Socrates and Virgil as lovers, of which—as "E. K." suggests—many were scandalous. Burton in *The Anatomy of Melancholy* (Shilleto's edition, I: 44) amused himself by making a collection of the scandalous examples. It is to Burton that we must look for a hint of the inwardness of Spenser's reminiscence of the contempt of Virgil's Alexis for the rustic Corydon as well as for the key to the associative process which made "E. K." introduce his labored note in defense of Virgil's reputation. The allusion to the "Alexis" was a commonplace whenever discussion turned upon an unrequited friendship. "Democritus Junior" used it in his analysis of friendlessness as a cause of melancholy. "I give, I bribe," he wrote, perhaps remembering poor Hobbinol's case, "I send presents, but they are refused. *Rusticus est [sic] Corydon nec munera curat Alexis*. I protest, I swear, I weep . . . . *odioque rependit amores, Irrisu lachrymas* . . . ." (Part III, Section ii, Member 5, Subsection 5.)

Virgil's line, *Rusticus es*, etc., echoed in the minds of all educated men in the Renaissance with the familiarity born of youthful construing in the grammar schools. It must have been quoted of many an aging don who watched the generations of "university wits" leave Cambridge and Oxford for London. It is a curious bond between Spenser's personal allegory in the *Calendar* and Virgil's in the *Eclogues*—real but fortuitous.

ELIZABETH

Elusively among the shadows in Virgil's allegory moves the figure of Augustus. He is the god of Tityrus' grateful piety in the first Eclogue.

> O Meliboee, deus nobis haec otia fecit.
> —Line 6.

He is the deity celebrated by Menalcas in the fifth Eclogue.

> Ipsa sonant arbusta: deus, deus ille, Menalca!
> —Line 64.

Here DeWitt sees (*Biographia*, p. 148) a reminiscence of Virgil's first meeting with Augustus. Mackail suggests (*Virgil*, p. 35) the possibility that the two men may have been friends since their school days together under the rhetorician, Epidius. Certainly they were united by their attachment to the cause of Italian prosperity. We should hardly expect to find traces of a relation like theirs in the pastorals of any continental poet of the Renaissance (with the possible exception of Petrarch writing to Cola de Rienzi) and in fact we do not find anything resembling their relation in the tone of tactfully familiar compliment which Ronsard taught to the poets of the *Pléiade* by his example in the "Bocage Royal" and in his *Eclogues*. But Spenser, we might expect, would have the idealistic attitude of Virgil toward Augustus for his Queen. Such, no doubt, would have been his attitude if he had not been entangled with Leicester and the Puritan movement when he was at work on the *Calendar*. He seems to have written it in the mood which he expressed in *Mother Hubberds Tale*. To that mood we may owe the fact that he composed only one "Aeglogue purposely intended to the honour and praise of [his] most gracious sovereign, Queen Elizabeth." This was "April." It owes absolutely nothing to Virgil's pastorals but Spenser appended to it the two Virgilian emblems, *Quam te memorem, virgo*, for Thenot, and for Hobbinol, *O dea certe.* "E. K." glossed them punctiliously:

This poesye is taken out of Virgile, and there of him used in the person of Aeneas to his mother Venus, appearing to him in likenesse of one of Dianaes damosells: being there most divinely set forth. To which similitude of divinitie Hobbinol comparing the excelency of Eliza, and being through the worthynes of Colins song, as it were, overcome with the hugenesse of his imagination, brusteth out in great admiration, (*O quam te memorem virgo?*) being otherwise unhable, then by suddein silence to expresse the worthinesse of his conceipt. Whom Thenot answereth with another part of the like verse, as confirming by his graunt and approvaunce, that Elisa is no whit inferiour to the majestie of her of whome that poete so boldly pronounced *O dea certe.*

These two tags of Latin were sure to be recognized by every reader of the *Calendar* as coming from Aeneas' speech of recognition of his mother in the First Book of the *Aeneid*.

               Veneris contra sic filius orsus:
Nulla tuarum audita mihi neque visa sororum,
  O—quam te memorem, virgo? namque haud tibi vultus
Mortalis, nec vox hominem sonat: O, dea certe.
                      —Lines 325–328.

Because everyone would instantly recognize the allusion to the *Aeneid*, this compliment carried a heavy freight of that "auctoritie" so ardently craved by

"E. K." Modern students would like to know how much additional "auctoritie" it may have gained unconsciously from the use of the same quotations in the masques and entertainments of which so many were given in Elizabeth's honor. The emblems of almost all the eclogues in the *Calendar* confess their copybook origin, and we may be sure that those attached to "April" were written in the commonplace books of all the Public Orators at Cambridge from Gabriel Harvey to George Herbert. One instance of the dramatic use of the recognition scene in the First Book of the *Aeneid*, manifestly as a compliment to the Queen, has survived in the first act of Marlowe's *Dido, Queen of Carthage*. (Everyman edition, p. 335.) Marlowe's treatment of the incident implies a public already familiar with it. Spenser's use of the same scene from the *Aeneid* in the Second Book of *The Faerie Queene* (II, iii: 21–31), again in open allusion to Elizabeth, justifies the suspicion that his fondness for this particular Virgilian passage was based upon a widespread appreciation of its aptness for compliment to the Virgin Queen. In spite of his use of two tags of verse from Virgil as keystones in his personal allegory in the *Calendar*, Spenser learned nothing directly about the management of such an allegory from Virgil, and the comparisons which he invites serve only to make us keenly conscious of the contrast between the personal friendships shadowed in the two collections of pastoral poetry.

III

The Ghost of Virgil's Pastoral World

To Thomas Warton in 1754 Spenser's pastoral world seemed like a province colonized from Virgil's. With the opening of the first Eclogue—

> Tityre, tu patulae recubans sub tegmine fagi
> Silvestrem tenui Musam meditaris avena;
> Nos patriae finis et dulcia linquimus arva:
> Nos patriam fugimus; tu, Tityre, lentus in umbra
> Formosam resonare doces Amaryllida silvas.

Warton compared the first stanza in "June":

HOBBINOL.
> Lo! Colin, here the place whose pleasaunt syte
> From other shades hath weand my wandering minde:
> Tell me, what wants me here to worke delyte?
> The simple ayre, the gentle warbling wynde,
> So calme, so coole, as nowhere else I fynde
> The grassye ground with daintye daysies dight,
> The bramble bush, where byrds of every kynde
> To the waters fall their tunes attemper right.

Both passages sing the seductions of an earthly paradise, and in both the paradise is a symbol of escape from the slings and arrows of fortune. Hobbinol tries to entice Colin away from the disappointments of his post-academic career to the charm and security of Cambridge. Virgil's commentators are not agreed about the inwardness of the first Eclogue, but it undoubtedly contrasts the blessedness of those who are free to cultivate their own gardens with the harder lot of those less fortunate.

Since Warton's day we have discovered a new pastoral world with the help of Wordsworth, Thoreau, and Housman, and our criticism inquires whether Spenser's conception of nature as the background and subject of pastoral poetry corresponds with Virgil's conception. To sympathetic readers of the *Eclogues* it is clear that on this point there is an absolute contrast between the two men. Herford reminds us that Spenser "was born and nursed in the heart of London" and that "his memory was not, like Shakespeare's, stored with rural images"; while Nettleship interprets Virgil's mind mainly in the light of his rural birth and of the sympathy which it gave him with the land.[10] Greg opens his volume on pastoral poetry and pastoral drama by observing that Spenser's contemporaries conceived the "nature" which their pastorals portrayed as a pleasing contrast to the town. As a positive element of experience it did not enter their imaginations. Because it was a mere way of escape from "the corruptions of an artificial civilization" it inevitably dressed itself in the innocence and luscious beauty of an Eden. The sentimental treatment of nature became a poetic principle. Sannazaro and Ronsard in their prefaces to their pastorals professed a naïf primitivism which might have passed muster with Rousseau. Their theory, supplemented by the idea of "decorum" as "E. K." expounded it in his letter to Gabriel Harvey, was responsible for the flatness of the rustic characters and atmosphere in the *Calendar*. Sannazaro's remarks occur in the prose essay prefixed to the *Arcadia*:

[10] *Vide* the introduction to Herford's edition of the *Calendar*, p. xvi, and Nettleship's *Essay on the poetry of Virgil*, where he finds (p. 33) "many a reminiscence of Virgil's early years in the *Georgics*, where his love of the woods in which he wandered as a boy meets one on every page." Miss Lilly's *The Georgic* summarizes (pp. 10–13) the traditional, the scientific, and the personal elements in Virgil's feeling for nature.

Per la qual cosa ancora, siccome io stimo, addiviene, che le silvestre canzoni vergate nelle rievide corteccie di' faggi dilettino non meno a chi le legge, che le colti versi scritti nelle rase carte degl'indorati libri; e le incerate canne de'pastori porgano per le fiorite valli forse piu piacevole suono, che li tersi e pregiati bossi de' musici per le pompose camere non fanno.—*Arcadia*, ed. by Scherillo, pp. 1, 2.

Ronsard reproduced the spirit of this passage in the opening lines of his first *Eclogue*:

> Des libres oiselets plus doux est la ramage,
> Que n'est le chant contraint du Rossignol en cage,
> Et la source d'une eau saillante d'un rocher,
> Est plus doux au passant pour le soif estancher
> (Quand sans art elle coule en sa rive rustique)
> Que n'est une fontaine en marbre magnifique,
> Iallissant par effort en un tuyau doré
> Au milieu de la cour d'un Palais honoré.
> Plus belle est une Nymphe en sa cotte agrafée,
> Aux coudes demy-nuds, qu'une Dame coifée
> D'artifice soigneux, toute peinte de fard:
> Car tousjours la nature est meilleure que l'art.
>
> Pource ie me promets que le chant solitaire
> Des sauuages Pasteurs doit d'auantage plaire
> (D'autant qu'il est naïf, sans art & sans façon)
> Qu'une plus curieuse & superbe chanson
> De ces maistres enflez d'une Muse hardie,
> Qui font trembler le ciel sous une tragedie,
> Et d'un vers ampoullé d'une effroyable vois
> Redoublent le malheur des Princes & des Rois.
> —Laumonier's edition, III: 356–57.

To this half-serious primitivism the sincerity of Virgil's pleasure in nature is quite alien. Pastoral poets in the sixteenth century could revive the motifs of Virgil's bucolic poetry, but they could not give to them the tone of experience made actual which pervades the *Eclogues* and *Georgics.* Even in passages which merely—Whitman-like—catalogue the pleasures of a rural life, Virgil never loses his sense of personal identification with his theme.

> At secura quies et nescia fallere vita,
> Dives opum variarum, at latis otia fundis,
> Speluncae, vivique lacus, at frigida Tempe,
> Mugitusque boum, mollesque sub arbore somni
> Non absunt; illic saltus ac lustra ferarum,
> Et patiens operum exiguoque adsueta iuventus,
> Sacra deum, sanctique patres.
> —*Georgics*, II: 467–73.

When he represents the *otia* of pastoral scenes and the golden happiness of an Epicurean returning to some *Noctes Albae* in the Apennines, Virgil never descends from emotion to sentimentality. "He had a more intimate union of soul with the soul of mountains and woodland than is granted to common generations of men," says Sellar apropos of the great lyric passages in the *Georgics:*

> Vos sylvae amnesque Lycaei . . . .
> Vocat alta voce Cythaeron . . . .

and

> O, ubi campi
> Sperchaeusque, et virginibus bacchata Lacaenis
> Taygeta . . . .

Spenser has no nostalgia for Mount Taygeta and no yearning suspicion that

> Fortunatus et ille, deos qui novit agrestis,
> Panaque Silvanumque senem Nymphasque sorores.
> —*Georgics*, II: 494–95.

He has no real peasants and no interest in rural life except a doctrinaire's fancy that high thinking and plain living flourish in the great open spaces. Thomalin, in "July," exemplifies Spenser's theory and finally crystallizes it in the copybook maxim assigned as his emblem, *In medio virtus*. The golden mean seems necessarily to have involved retirement to the country in the manner of the disillusioned courtier, Meliboeus, in the sixth book of *The Faerie Queene*. Even after long experience, Meliboeus remains academic in his preference for the country over the town. "Wisedome is most riches" Spenser makes the burden of his sermon to Sir Calidore. Virgil's gentleman farmer knew better than Meliboeus when, and why, he was well off.

> Hic focus et taedae pingues, hic plurimus ignis
> Semper, et assidua postes fuligine nigri;
> Hic tantum Boreae curamus frigora, quantum
> Aut numerum lupus, aut torrentia flumina ripas.
> —*Eclogues*, VII: 49–52.

The Shepheardes Calendar has no trace of Virgil's power to realize the emotions evoked by the changing face of nature. Though it pretended to reflect the seasons, the *Calendar* never escaped in its treatment of them from either the pathetic fallacy on the one hand or frigid conventionality on the other. Spenser was satisfied to write within the confines of the attitude set up by Sannazaro and Ronsard. He simply did not and could not possibly have the comprehension of peasant life which expresses itself in books like the *Georgics* and *North of Boston*. Doubtless, he sympathized entirely with his contemporary, Harington, in the latter's confession[11] that he could not endure to hear his ploughmen talk of twyfallowing, while he adored the elegance of Virgil's

> Saepe etiam steriles incendere profuit agros.

We look in vain in the *Calendar* for a passage like that in the third Georgic (vv. 322-30) where Virgil recalls the intimate emotions associated with lengthening days in the spring on an Italian farm.

The most striking indication that *The Shepheardes Calendar* owes nothing of significance to Virgil is the fact that it took over nothing from the *Georgics*.[12] French pastoral poetry appropriated widely—though conventionally—from them. Peletier translated the first *Georgic* in 1547. Baïf and Ronsard show many echoes of them. In Italy they were much imitated in such work as Giovanni Rucellai's *Le Api* and Luigi Alamanni's *Coltivazione*. In Spain translation of them began as early as 1574.[13] In England there was no translation before 1589, and, perhaps because agriculture was yielding to sheep-raising, there seems to have been little interest in the *Georgics*. Only one point of contact between them and *The Shepheardes*

---

[11] In the preface to his translation of the "Orlando Furioso," in *Elizabethan Critical Essays*, II: 206.

[12] Renwick, *Spenser*, p. 56, suggests that perhaps "some such notion" as that of imitating the *Georgics* "lay behind the topographical poem on the rivers of England, the *Epithalamion Thamesis* mentioned in Spenser's second letter to Harvey and afterward recast as Canto XI of the Fourth Book of *The Faerie Queene*." Mr. Renwick says that although the teaching of Spenser's poem was "informative and intellectual . . . . as distinct from moral and spiritual, ... such teaching had the authority of the master, and topography is as respectable a study as agriculture. If the mind of Augustan Italy needed to be attracted to the fields, so was it the duty of the Englishman, conscious of his nationality in a time of rising patriotism, to know his England, and the marriage-song of the Thames could be wrought into a panegyric of that many-watered land as properly as the *Georgics* into the praise of Virgil's

'Magna parens frugum, Saturnia tellus.' "

[13] *Vide* Menendez y Pelayo's introduction to his *Eglogas y Georgicas*, edited by D. Felix M. Hidalgo and Miguel A. Caro, pp. xii-xiii.

Calendar has been suggested (by Riedner, *Belesenheit*, p. 17) and that will serve to betray the contrast between the attitudes of the two poets. Virgil's *Pan, ovium custos*, according to the letter, seems identical with Spenser's

> .... sovereigne Pan! thou god of shepheardes all,
> Which of our tender lambkins takest keepe,
> And, when our flocks into mischaunce maught fall,
> Doest save from mischiefe the unwary sheepe,
> Als of their maisters hast no lesse regarde,
> Then of the flocks, which thou doest watch and warde.
> —"December," vv. 7–12.

According to the spirit, Virgil's deity is centuries away from this. Boccaccio in the *Bucolicum Carmen* established the convention of using the name ambiguously to mean both the Christian and the Arcadian divinities. Marot, in the lines which Spenser was translating in the stanza quoted, was beginning the fashion of referring by it to a living monarch.

> O Pan Dieu souverain,
> Qui de guarder ne fus onc paresseux
> Parcs et brebis et les maistres d'iceux.

Pan, in the fantastic autobiographical maze of *December*, is a deity of conflicting attributes; half mere god of shepherds whom Spenser in his inspired days—like another Apollo—shamed in a music-match, and half over-arching Providence which the repentant Spenser flatters with his *confessio amantis*. In the distinction between the chameleon Pan of the *Calendar* and the Pan of the *Georgics* whom Virgil treated with piety as the embodiment of the spirit to which the work was dedicated, we have a symbol of the gulf dividing Spenser's conception of "nature" and his pastoral world from those of Virgil.

IV
"E. K's" Critical Authority

The testimony of Spenser's contemporaries about the relation of his pastorals to Virgil's *Eclogues* and *Georgics* is scanty and hardly unanimous. "E. K's" references in his glosses to the Greek pastoral poets justify the presumption that he was not familiar with Theocritus, Bion, and Moschus. Indeed we are almost certain that he had read them only in translated fragments. This is not true of his knowledge of Virgil. His annotations prove a wide, though inaccurate acquaintance with Virgil's poetry. He noticed all the verbal tangencies between *The Shepheardes Calendar* and the *Eclogues* which have figured in the present essay. In his zeal, he even noticed as Virgilian some lines which have no analogues anywhere in Virgil. Two of these Mr. Mustard has explained and justified[14] as coming from the pseudo-Virgilian *De Musis*. Another note of "E. K." was still less happy. Anent Spenser's groaning oak in "February" (v. 215) he applauded, "a livelye figure, whiche geveth sence and feeling to unsensible creatures, as Virgile also sayeth: 'Saxa gemunt gravido'." The phrase cited does not occur anywhere in Virgil's works or in the pseudo-Virgiliana. Similarly unlucky was his note on "May" (v. 205) where he made the quaint suggestion that when Spenser's mother goat says to her kid,

---
[14] In *"E. K's" Classical Allusions*, p. 198. With "April," v. 111, "E. K." compared the line,
   Signat cuncta manu, loquitur Polyhymnia gestu,
and with "November," v. 53,
   Melpomene Tragico proclamat maesta boatu.

> .... so thy Father his head upheld
> And so his dainty hornes did he weld!

she was echoing Andromache in the *Aeneid* (III: 490) when, seeing Ascanius and remembering that Astyanax had been of the same age, Andromache exclaims,

> Sic oculos, sic ille manus, sic ora ferebat.

Akin to this is the far-fetched allusion to Circe,

> Dea saeva potentibus herbis, &c.

in the gloss to "December" (v. 88), as proof that there was good and ancient authority for Spenser's hope—like Milton's in *Il Penseroso*—that "tryed time" might teach him

> The power of herbs, both which can hurt and ease.

Perhaps there was just a trace of the medieval deification of Virgil in "E. K's" mind. He quaintly made Virgil the court of last resort in mythologico-literary matters. In his note on "April" (v. 100) he proved that Calliope is not the Muse of Rhetoric because by Virgil "in hys Epigrams, that arte semeth to be attributed to Polymnia, saying,

> Signat cuncta manu loquiturque Polymnia gestu.

The lurking trace of superstition in "E. K's" veneration of Virgil has much to account for. His establishment of Spenser as "the English Maro" was accepted at once by almost all their contemporaries. Sidney's praise of the *Calendar* in the *Defence of Poesie* raised it to the rank of an English classic, and "E. K." became the captain of a file of goose-stepping followers. William Webbe in his *Discourse of English Poetry* (1586) preached the doctrine of imitation of the Greek and Latin classics and hailed the "new Poete" (i.e., Spenser, whose *incognito* was still officially preserved) for having acquitted himself well in that matter. Webbe himself set an example for all aspirants to pastoral honors by paraphrasing the first two of Virgil's *Eclogues*. Webbe's statement of the case for Spenser as a good Virgilian, however, is not impressive.

> Virgill hath a gallant report of Augustus covertly expressed in the first Aeglogue; the like is in him of her Majestye under the name of Eliza. Virgill maketh a brave coloured complaint of unsteadfast friendshippe in the person of Corydon; the like is in him in his 5 Aeglogue. Agayne beholde the prettie Pastoral contentions of Virgill in the third Aeglogue; of him in the eight Aeglogue.
> —*Elizabethan Critical Essay*, I: 263.

Against the traditional drift of criticism by men to whom the imitation of the Classics was dangerously like a superstition Thomas Nash was the only person to raise his voice. In Spenser's experiments with English accentual meters in the *Calendar* he saw a revolt against the Virgilian hexameter and when attacking Gabriel Harvey in *Foure Letters confuted* (1592) he wrote:

> The Hexameter verse I graunt to be a Gentleman of an ancient house (so is many an English beggar); yet this Clyme of ours he cannot thrive in; our speech is too craggy for him to set his plough in; and he goes twitching and hopping in our language like a man running upon quagmiers, up the hill in one Syllable, and down the dale in another, retaining no part of that stately smooth gate, which he vaunts himself with amongst the Greeks and Latins.
>
> Homer and Virgill, two valourous Authors, yet were they never knighted, they wrote in Hexameter verses:

Ergo, Chaucer and Spenser, the Homer and Virgill of England, were farre overseene, that they wrote not all of their Poems in Hexamiter verses also.
—Bullen's edition, I: 298–99.

In his impudent stress upon Spenser's neglect of the classical verse, on the aptness of which for English poetry Harvey had staked his critical reputation, Nash was certainly on the track of the real tendency in the experimental patterns and rhythms of the *Calendar*. It seems to have been of set purpose that Spenser used lyric stanzas so much and riding rhyme so seldom. Mantuan, whose Latin pastorals counted for much with Spenser when he wrote the *Calendar*, used the hexameter, and Marot's *Eclogues* were all written in decasyllables. Spenser adapted and translated from both poets, but he was blind to their example in continuing the Virgilian measure as far as their respective *media* permitted. As we have seen, he joined Ronsard, Baïf, and Du Bellay in abandoning the Virgilian metrical tradition for the most part to experiment with a variety of narrative and lyric measures. Instead of conforming to the comparatively fixed standard of mass which held Virgil's *Eclogues* to a roughly constant length, he made his pastorals sometimes almost as short as epigrams and sometimes almost as long as one-act plays. From the point of view of form, Nash was fully justified in suggesting that *The Shepheardes Calendar* was a revolt from the Virgilian tradition.

Spenser's poetic diction seems also to have been felt and probably to have been intended as deliberately un-Virgilian. In his complaint in the *Apology for Poetry* that Spenser neglected the authority of

Virgil and of Theocritus in framing "his style to an old, rustic language" Sidney wrote what must have been a commonplace of contemporary opinion. Among the continental critics there were two radically opposed views of Virgil's language, but there were no delusions on either side as to its being dialectic or archaic. Du Bellay noted that Virgil's archaisms were inset like gems and warned his readers that their value was a consequence of their rarity. (*Défence*, p. 129.) Trissino, on the other hand, as Miss Pope has pointed out (*P. M. L. A.*, XLI: p. 588.), systematized the principle of decorum and applied it to the diction of the pastoral. He half-apologized for the failure of Virgil and Theocritus to "preserve a decorum of language" and extolled Strassino and Batista Soardo as pioneers in the use of dialect. Ronsard sympathized (*Art poétique*, p. 333) with Trissino. In England critical feeling leaned against the use of dialect, and Puttenham joined Sidney in disallowing "the terms of Northernmen . . . , though no man can deny that theirs is the purer English Saxon at this day, yet it is not so courtly nor so currant as our Southerne English is; no more is the far Westerne mans speech." (Quoted by Renwick, *Spenser*, p. 84.) Spenser in *The Shepheardes Calendar*, no doubt much to the subsequent delight of the author of *Have with you to Saffron Walden*, joined the innovators in language and rejected the conservative prejudices of those who wished to make Virgil a pattern of either meter or diction.

Conclusion

"E. K." has emerged from our discussion as a commentator with less discretion than zeal for establishing "the new poet's" bond with the great names in the pastoral tradition, among which Virgil was—in sixteenth-century eyes—the greatest. He can hardly be blamed for that, grotesque or impertinent though every observation which it led him to make may have seemed under our scrutiny. Spenser himself—as we shall soon find—encouraged comparison of *The Faerie Queene* with the *Aeneid* very much as "E. K." had done between the *Calendar* and the *Eclogues*. Together they established a dogma in English literary criticism which flourished as late as Dryden's *Essay on Satire* and is not extinct even today. Yet—so far as the *Calendar* is concerned—the dogma deserves to survive only as a curiosity in the history of criticism. Virgil's influence upon the *Calendar* seems to have been slight, indirect, and distorted. It is impossible to put the finger on a single passage in Spenser's pastorals and say, "Here, beyond a doubt, the poet's *imagination* was set alight by his reading of Virgil."

Incidentally, however, we have found one point in "August," in the descriptive art of the carved scene on Willye's cup, where it seems almost certain that Spenser's imagination was kindled by Ronsard. "August" as a whole has taken its place for us as one of a group of poems—perhaps, though not necessarily, written by men who were successively acquainted with one another's work—in which four of Virgil's motifs obstinately survived while his rhythm was discarded. We have watched the four motifs pass through the successive metamorphoses of irresponsible experiment, burlesque, and satire in the hands of Baïf, Spenser, Sidney, and Hall.

In the subtler matters of Spenser's allegory and artistic purpose no genuine Virgilian influence has come to light. We have only a few scattered proofs in verbal parallels that Spenser preserved clear memories of the *Eclogues*, and some of these are as grotesque as the strange echoes of Dante in Chaucer's *House of Fame*. Our interest in them is psychological rather than literary. The problem is to unravel the associative processes behind Spenser's use of the emblem, *Quam te memorem, virgo*?

Spenser was an eager experimenter in the *Calendar* and it was in that spirit that he believed every pastoral poet set to work. He could sympathize with the pleasure of the craftsmen in France and Italy who were giving intricacy and polish to their verses, but a poetic career begun as Robert Frost began his with *North of Boston* or as Virgil began his with the *Eclogues* must have been a closed mystery to Spenser. Of all the pastoral poets whose "auctoritie" "E. K." cited in his defense, Virgil was the only one whom Spenser's nature and education positively unfitted him to understand.

VIRGILS GNAT

An Interchapter

The unique position of *Virgils Gnat* among Spenser's works seems to indicate that in an essay of this kind it should be studied in a short interchapter. The English poem is avowedly a translation from the Latin. It has the semblance of a literary exercise although it may have had a less innocent intention. As a verse translation it has the virtue of accuracy rather excessively, but that fact may not be significant of Spenser's powers or attitude as a translator. If he was Englishing the *Culex* with a perilous purpose in mind, he would be tempted to screen himself by exaggerated fidelity to his original.

Spenser's rendering is more diffuse than seems desirable to our taste, but by the standards of his contemporaries it must have seemed exceptionally faithful to both the form and spirit of the Latin. Spenser relaxed his vigilant accuracy only twice; once in the description of Tartarus and again in the catalogue of flowers which are heaped on the tomb of the murdered gnat. In both of these cases he seems to have "risen to his theme" and the results are interesting because they appear to have been faintly influential in *The Faerie Queene*. Several of the phrases and images in the *Gnat* lived in Spenser's memory to recur in his record of the scenes traversed by Duessa and Night on their infernal journey in the fifth canto of his First Book. Virgil's description of Cerberus gave Spenser a stanza which left a distinct echo in the following lines from the First Book, as comparison of the three passages shows:

Cerberus et diris flagrant latratibus ora; Anguibus hinc atque hinc horrent cui colla reflexis Sanguineique micant ardorem luminis orbes. —Lines 220–22.	And Cerberus whose many mouthes doo bay, And barke out flames, as if on fire he fed; Adowne whose necke, in terrible array, Ten thousand snakes cralling about his hed, Doo hang in heapes that horribly affray, And bloodie eyes doo glister firie red; He oftentimes me dreadfully doth threaten, With painfull torments to be sorely beaten. —Lines 345–52.

Before the threshold dreadfull Cerberus
His three deformed heads did lay along,
Curled with thousand adders venemous,
And lilled forth his bloody flaming tong.
—I, v: 34.

The allusion to Tityus in the following stanza,

And Tityus fed a vulture on his maw,

may also be a recollection of the *Gnat:*

Et Tityos Latona, tuae memor anxius irae (Implacabilis ira nimis) iacet alitis esca. Terreor, a tantis insistere terreor umbris, Ad Stygias revocatus aquas. —Lines 237–40.	And there is mournfull Tityus mindfull yet Of thy displeasure, O Latona faire; Displeasure too implacable was it That made him meate for wild foules of the ayre: Much do I feare among such fiends to sit; Much do I feare back to them to repayre, To the black shadowes of the Stygian shore, Where wretched ghosts sit wailing evermore. —Lines 377–84.

In the scattered resemblances to the fifth canto of Book One of *The Faerie Queene* which it is not altogether fanciful to see in the latter part of the *Gnat*, there is evidence that the canto was written at about the time when Spenser made his translation of the *Culex*. The sonnet which dedicates the *Gnat* to Leicester indicates that it was written late in the period of Spenser's connection with him, perhaps in 1580. The Spenser-Harvey correspondence proves the existence of some part of an *Elvish Queene* at an even earlier date. Perhaps a draught of the fifth canto of Spenser's First Book was written at the very time when he was translating the *Culex*.

Spenser's description in *Virgils Gnat* of the world beyond the grave seems like an attenuated shadow of Dante's hell, and has no resemblance to the inferno in the sixth *Aeneid*. Virgil's hell in the *Culex*, says DeWitt (*Virgil's Biographia Literaria*, p. 17), "a mere catalogue without visual imagination or geography, is pure boyish pedantry." While the *Gnat* anticipates most of Spenser's later treatments of the legends of the damned in the glimpses of the infernal world in *The Faerie Queene*, it contributed nothing to his conception of the physical aspect of hell. His descriptions of the infernal realms in Book One, canto five, and in Book Two, canto seven, owe nothing to the *Culex*.

Virgil ended his poem with a catalogue of the flowers piled upon the grave of the murdered gnat by the remorseful shepherd. Spenser expanded the flower passage into his twenty-four final lines. DeWitt, who sees in Virgil's mock elegy only the pedantic trifling of a seventeen-year-old boy, is inclined to look at the whole performance as a mistake of his adolescence. Frank sees in it a maturity and a purpose which relate it closely to Spenser's paraphrase—if there is truth in the theory that *Virgils Gnat* was an allegory addressed to Leicester, and that Leicester is the shepherd saved by the insect's sting from the serpent's bite, while Spenser is the gnat crushed for its pains. If the *Culex* was addressed to Augustus, it is hard to avoid the conclusion that it contains a personal allegory resembling that of Spenser's translation. Frank believes that it was intended for the Emperor and suggests that in "the long list of flowers so incongruously massed on the gnat's grave, and in the two hundred lines that detail the ghostly census of Hades" (*Virgil, a Biography*, p. 32) there were reminiscences of the lectures which Virgil and Octavian had heard together from their teacher, Epidius. If Frank is right, Spenser's paraphrase of the *Culex* is one of the happiest examples of apt appropriation from classical literature in the Renaissance.

The Virgilian *Culex* had had a long history of translations, editions, and commentaries on the Continent before Spenser was attracted to it. In 1572 Scaliger summed up the results of more than fifty years of study of the *Culex* by various scholars in his *Publii Virgilii appendix* (Lyon). Immediately afterwards there began a series of popular and school editions of which Stigel's, "studiosi juventutis gratia," and Ascencius' *Familiaris expositio* (1574)[25] were the first. The earliest publication of the *Culex* was in the second printed edition of Virgil, the *Romana Altera* of 1471, edited by Giovanni Andrea Bussi, Bishop of Aléria. The first Aldine edition to contain it was printed at Venice in 1505. After that date

---

[25] *Vide* Plésent, *Le Culex*, pp. 35–48, for a complete list of editions of the poem during and since the fifteenth century. There were no English editions during Spenser's lifetime.

the number of editions was, in the words of the latest editor of the poem, M. Charles Plésent, "tel que vouloir dresser une liste complète serait un travail aussi fastidieux qu'inutile" (*Le Culex*, p. 35). Side by side with the ordinary texts ran a series of illustrated editions which began in 1502, one of which may have been responsible for some of the verbal embroidery which adds more than three hundred lines in Spenser's paraphrase to the length of the original poem.

In his youth Cardinal Bembo made the *Culex* the subject of a witty philological dialogue which became famous in Italy, the *De Virgilii Culice et Terentii Fabulis* (1530). Under cover of his dramatic fiction Bembo edited the text, proposed numerous conjectural alterations, not all of them happy, and dealt at large with his own personal ideas about philology and about the future of the humanities in Italy. Although he was an uncompromising Ciceronian, Bembo honored his master in the spirit rather than in the letter of this dialogue. He introduced himself and his friend, Girolamo Quirino, talking together one summer afternoon beside the church of Santa Maria della Minerva in a racy sixteenth-century Latin that was not quite the dialect of the *Tusculans*. Both the dialogue and the *Culex* which was embedded in it became famous. Professor Oliver Emerson (*Jour. of Eng. and Ger. Phil.*, XVII: 94–118) has made it clear that many of Bembo's emendations found their way into the edition of the *Culex* which Spenser used, and there is a presumption that he was familiar with the Cardinal's dialogue.

Spenser's translation was annotated in a hostile spirit by Jortin in the early part of the eighteenth century, and it has been defended against his strictures with great erudition by Professor Emerson. The latter's article furnishes a complete apparatus of notes. It replies to all Jortin's criticisms, line by line, refuting virtually all of them by showing that Spenser's rendering of the Latin was justified by Bembo's rather corrupt text. My own examination of Bembo's dialogue edition shows two or three insignificant variations by Spenser from the readings that he recommended. For example, Bembo ended by arguing (pp. 814–16) that in the eighth line from the end of the text as he had it—

>   Buphthalamusque virens, & semper florida Picris

—the last word should read "Pinus." Spenser evidently read "Picris," for he translated the line:

>   Oxeye still greene, and bitter patience. (678)

It is still a question whether the translation of the *Culex* indicates that Spenser had any particular interest in Virgil apart from the juvenile poem which happened very conveniently to enable him to hide a daring claim upon Leicester's gratitude behind the double mask of allegory and of translation from an ancient poet. However, it is a striking fact that Spenser was attracted by both of Virgil's minor epics, the *Culex* and the *Ciris*, to make a complete translation of the one and to reproduce a part of the other (as we shall find) in *The Faerie Queene*. The elements in them which attracted him were perhaps the artificiality of ornament, the "Alexandrianism" which Virgil discarded, but the freedom of their epic style may have helped him to achieve in the *Gnat* a syntax and a cadence which begins to resemble that of *The Faerie Queene*.

PART II

THE EPIC AND THE ROMANCE

THE EPIC AND THE ROMANCE

I

"The English Virgil"

But in no *Iliad* let the youth engage
His tender years, and unexperienced age;
Let him by just degrees and steps proceed,
Sing with the swains and tune the tender reed:
He with success a humble theme may ply,
And, Virgil-like, immortalize a fly.
—Vida, *Art of Poetry*, p. 637.

There was no mere coincidence in the fact that the growth of the poetic mind began with Spenser as it did with Virgil in the tender reed and the immortalization of a fly. It began in the same way with most of the poets who made the French and Italian renaissance. As "E. K." intimated, it could decently begin in no other way. Spenser, said "E. K.," in writing *The Shepheardes Calendar*, was

following the example of the best and most auncient poetes, which devised this kind of wryting, being both so base for the matter, and homely for the manner, at the first to trye theyr habilities, and, as young birdes that be newly crept out of the nest, by little first to prove theyr tender wyngs, before they make a greater flyght. So flew Theocritus, as you may perceive he was all ready full fledged. So flew Virgile, as not yet well feeling his winges. So flew Mantuane, as being not full somd. So Petrarque. So Boccace. So Marot, Sannazarus, and also divers other excellent both Italian and French poetes, whose foting this author every where followeth.

When Spenser made his début with the eclogues which everywhere followed the footing of Virgil and obscurely promised an epic flight to come, he was as much the passive subject of a great law of literature in the sixteenth century as he was an active disciple of Virgil. The law had its roots as strongly fixed in social conditions as in literary tradition. The vogue of the pastoral tempted young men to experiment with eclogues, and the fast developing self-consciousness of nations and of princes encouraged them to dream of writing epics. "De bonne heure," says Sainte-Beuve of Virgil (*Etude*, p. 52) in words which Spenser and many French and Italian poets of his time would have felt no presumption in applying to themselves, "le poète a l'aspiration aux grandes choses, aux grands sujets vers lesquels il se dirige dans sa calme et puissante douceur." Already when the *Calendar* was published, Spenser was at work upon an *Elvish Queene*. When the first part of *The Faerie Queene* appeared, it was prefaced with a stanza which every reader recognized at once as a translation of the famous lines linking the *Eclogues* and *Georgics* to the *Aeneid*—lines which we today are sure were not written by Virgil, but which, after Sperone Speroni's apology for them (*Dialoghi*, p. 271), were accepted as genuine and as supremely significant in the sixteenth century—

> Lo! I the man, whose Muse whylome did maske,
> As time her taught, in lowly shepheardes weeds,
> Am now enforst, a farre unfitter taske,
> For trumpets sterne to chaunge mine oaten reeds,
> And sing of knights and ladies gentle deeds.

The passage claims a kind of sonship to Virgil, but it also involuntarily proves a brotherhood with a host of Spenser's contemporaries. Camoens opened the *Lusiads* with a paraphrase of the pseudo-Virgilian autobiographical couplet[26] and Ronsard, whose ambition it was to be known as the French Virgil, might well have placed it at the head of the *Franciade*. Robert Greene boldly parodied it in the Prologue to *Aphonsus:*

>My hand, which used for to pen
>The praise of love and Cupid's peerless power,
>Will now begin to treat of bloody Mars,
>Of doughty deeds and bloody victories.

Phineas Fletcher, in *The Purple Island*, canonized Virgil and Spenser together for having both mounted from the pastoral to the epic:

>Two shepherds most I love with just adoring;
>That Mantuan swain who changed his slender reed
>To trumpet's martial voice and warre's loud roaring,
>From Corydon to Turnus derring-deed;
>   And next our home-bred Colin's sweetest firing;
>   Their steps not following close, but far admiring.
>To lackey one of these is all my pride's aspiring.
>   —VI. 5.

Since all Europe, from Lisbon to London, was emulating Virgil's apprenticeship in the pastoral as a discipline for writing epic poetry, Spenser's use of the pseudo-Virgilian couplet to open *The Faerie Queene* goes to indicate the extent of Virgil's prestige in general rather than the directness and power of his influence upon Spenser. There can be no doubt, however, that Spenser agreed with "E. K." in regarding himself as a good Virgilian. In "October" he adjured himself to

---

[26] Grant me a daring and sonorous tone,
Not as from flute or shepherd's reed might flow,
But from harmonious martial trumpet blown,
That fires the breast and flushes all the brow.
            —Burton's translation.

> Abandon then the base and viler clowne:
> Lyft up thyselfe out of the lowly dust,
> And sing of bloody Mars, of wars, of guists.
>
> (ll. 37–9)

Yet these lines, as Kluge (*Anglia*, III: 272) has pointed out, are a complacent rendering of Mantuan's advice to himself:

> Dic pugnas, dic gesta virum, dic proelia regum;
> vertere ad hos qui sceptra tenent, qui regna gubernant:
> Invenies qui te de sordibus eruat istis.

The heirs of Virgil were only too conscious that the poetic laborer was worthy of his hire. In *The Teares of the Muses* Spenser deplored the philistinism and illiberality of the great and in "October" he repeated Mantuan's plaint that

> Mecoenas is yclad in claye,
> And great Augustus long ygoe is dead.
>
> (ll. 61–2)

The cynical may suspect that the echo of the pseudo-Virgilian couplet in the quatrain that he prefixed to *The Faerie Queene* was not so much a promise to "aemulate and overgoe" Virgil as it was an assertion of the rights of one of Virgil's heirs to the patronage of the heirs of Augustus. Spenser rather encouraged that idea by the sonnet dedicatory which he addressed to Sir Francis Walsingham:

> That Mantuane poetes incompared spirit,
>   Whose girland now is set in highest place,
>   Had not Mecaenas, for his worthy merit,
>   It first advaunst to great Augustus grace,
> Might long, perhaps, have lien in silence bace,
>   Ne bene so much admir'd of later age.
>   This lowly Muse, that learns like steps to trace,
>   Flies for like aide unto your patronage;
> That are the great Mecaenas of this age.

Whatever the successors of Augustus may have thought of Spenser's claim upon their patronage, no one doubted that he was preeminently the heir of the ancients and of Virgil in particular. To Thomas Lodge he was "best read in ancient poetry," while some of his contemporaries "accounted him more a classical scholar than a poet."[27] Burton in *The Anatomy of Melancholy* was in the habit of alluding to Spenser as "our Virgil," while Chaucer was "our Homer." Burton's practice was an inheritance from the preceding generation. In Elizabethan criticism Spenser was usually paired conventionally with Virgil, although Carew, in *The Excellency of English*,[28] bracketed him with Lucan. Dryden handed on the tradition[29] which remains today very much as he left it. Miss Nitchie, writing in 1919, says[30] that Spenser and his contemporaries subscribed to the creed that "the ancients have anticipated us in almost everything, and in everything that they have anticipated they have done so well that the best chance of success is simply to imitate them." She adds that Spenser's contemporaries often limited "'the ancients' to little more than Virgil, both in connection with the pastoral, and, more especially, in relation to the epic, although each is tinged with the influence of Renaissance models as well."

[27] *Vide* Fletcher, *Jour. Eng. and Germ. Phil.*, II: 443.
[28] Smith's *Elizabethan Critical Essay*, II: 293.
[29] *Essays of John Dryden* (ed. Ker), II: 28–29.
[30] *Virgil and the English Poets*, p. 9.

II
Epic vs. Romance

A flank attack upon the venerable tradition which Miss Nitchie has reconsecrated has been made by Professor Draper.[31] He objects that there was "little or no direct influence of the classics upon Spenser's narrative technique," and believes that it was primarily the example of Malory which determined the form given to *The Faerie Queene*. As a matter of literary history seen in the perspective in which it appears today, Malory's example may have eclipsed all others, both ancient and contemporary, for Spenser. We may be sure, however, that he was not aware of the fact as we are, and that he regarded the plan of his poem as sufficiently classical. His illusion was a natural effect of the influence of the Italian poetry and criticism which he ardently loved.

In his study of the sources of the *Orlando Furioso*, Pio Rajna distinguished three stages in the infiltration of classical influence upon Italian romance. They are represented respectively by the work of Boiardo and of Berni, of Ariosto, and of Tasso. In the multiplicity of plots, the comparative formlessness, and the predominant tendency to derive structure and material from the romances of Amadis, Tristram, and Charlemagne rather than from the classical epics, Rajna found reason for classing the *Orlando Innamorato* and its *rifacimenti* with medieval literature. They represent a time when contact with the classics was even

---

[31] "The Narrative Technique of *The Faerie Queene*," *P. M. L. A.*, XXXIX: 314.

weaker than it had been during the lifetime of Dante.[32] With the *Orlando Furioso* the return to the classic spirit began.

Il culmine vero nella storia del romanzo cavalleresco italiano è rappresentato dal primo, anziche dal secondo *Orlando*. Col poema del Conte di Scandiano ha termine lo svolgimento naturale e spontaneo del genere. Col *Furioso*, nato di padre italiano, ma di madre latina, incomincia nella stirpe un altro ramo, che, se riconosce ancora tra i suoi antenati la *Chanson de Roland* e il *Roman de Tristram*, deriva nondimeno buona parte del suo sangue dall'*Eneide*, dalle *Metamorfosi*, dalla *Tebaide*.
—*Le Fonti dell'Orlando Furioso*, p. 39.

Rajna does not at all mean that Ariosto complied *imaginatively* with the principles underlying the *Aeneid*.

Nell'Ariosto .... l'artista è sommo; quanto a correttezza di disegno, egli si lascia indietro a grandissima distanza il suo *predecessore;* ma in lui la conoscenza dei Classici non si transforma piu tutta in forza viva; al processo di ricreazione si sostituisce spesso l'imitazione.
—*Fonti*, p. 37.

Ariosto's debt to Virgil consisted in the appropriation of a number of incidents and details. Sometimes he took whole incidents of first-rate importance, like the story of Nisus and Euryalus, but his conception of plot remained un-Virgilian and corresponded to that of the later cyclical romances. The analogy with Spenser's perhaps involuntary reproduction of the

[32] Boiardo derived much of his material from the classics, especially from Ovid, but he destroyed the spirit of his sources as Ariosto did not. "Ogni episodio, classico o meno, che venga ridotto alla sua parte schematica è privato del movimento interno, che lo caratterizza, facilmente rientra a trovare posto nel campo dell'inventiva, avida di spunti, di situazioni, di colori nuovi." A. Azzolino. *Il Mondo Cavalleresco di Boiardo, Ariosto, Berni*, p. 216.

technique of *Le Morte d'Arthur* is obvious. Italian criticism after Ariosto was unanimous in approving his narrative technique and in asserting for it Aristotelian sanction.

A loose structure of almost any type (says Draper) (*op. cit.*, pp. 320–21), was permitted or even advocated; and Aristotle's allowance of episodic material was stretched to the limit. Scaliger, for instance, held the view that several plots ("fabulae"), each developed in a separate book or canto, form, in this combination, a complete epic. Trissino claimed epic unity for the *Decamerone* because (as in *The Faerie Queene*) all the stories are related to a basic situation and are consequently placed in a single frame. Giraldi Cinthio, moreover, in defending the *romanzi*, declared that they treated of "one or more illustrious actions of one or more excellent men"; he found tolerance, if not sanction, for such a scheme in Aristotle; and, like Spenser, commended it for the opportunity that it gave for episodic digression.

Ariosto's influence upon Spenser's structure and upon almost all the other elements of *The Faerie Queene* was so great that the features which he has in common with both Virgil and Spenser must be carefully discounted in appraising Spenser's debt to the *Aeneid*. Boiardo, on the other hand, is quite negligible as an intermediary between Virgil and Spenser.[33] About the influence of the *Gerusalemme*

---

[33] Blanchard in "Spenser and Boiardo" indicates nothing in common between the two which is derived from Virgil. Upton suggested that Boiardo's story of the kidnapping of Ricciardetto in *Orlando Innamorato*, I, iv, 97, may be an intermediary between Virgil's allusion to Tyrrhene Tarchon, who

ab equo dextra complectitur hostem
Et gremium ante suum multa vi concitus aufert.
—*Aeneid*, XI, 743–44

and Spenser's tale of Argante and Satyrane.

Liberata there is room for no real doubt. Draper says simply that it "was published too late seriously to have affected Spenser's plan," and Koeppel, writing in 1889, held the same opinion.[34] Tasso himself, in spite of his determination to achieve a genuinely classical unity in the *Gerusalemme*, was a champion of episodic structure and defended it out of the classics themselves. Writing to Scipio Gonzaga on the fifteenth of October, 1575, he said that his own practice in the *Goffredo* must be acceptable to "chi vuol salvar tutti gli Episodii dell'Odissea, e dell'Eneide,"[35] and boldly added that wherever he had allowed himself liberties not justified by Homer and Virgil, he did so because his art was finer than theirs. His editor, Beni, opened his edition of the *Gerusalemme* with a salvo of sonnets all replying with a unanimous "None" to the rhetorical question which closed the last of them:

> Qual'altro mai tanto avanzossi? O quale
> Fù ne la Grecia o pur nel Latio, stile
> Canuto sì? qual ne l'Etruria pari?

It is in the light of this criticism of Tasso that we should read Spenser's boyish avowal to Gabriel Harvey that he hoped to overgo Ariosto and all his predecessors

---

[33] *con.*   And on his collar laying puissant hand,
Out of his wavering seat him pluckt perforse,
Perforse him pluckt, unable to withstand,
Or help himselfe, and laying thwart her horse,
In loathly wise like to a carrion corse,
She bore him fast away.   (III, vii, 43)

The Spenserian scene appears to owe its origin to Boiardo, but it is just possible that Spenser's "puissant hand" is Virgil's "dextro" and that his "pluckt perforse, Perforse him pluckt" is Virgil's "direptum . . . . multa vi."

[34] "Für den plan der *F. Q.* hat es [*La Gerusalemme Liberata*] jedoch nur noch einer stelle als muster gedient, zu anfang der pastorale des Calidore (VI, 9)." (*Anglia*, XI: 343.)

[35] *Discorsi del S. Torquato Tasso sull'Arte et insieme il primo libro delle lettere*, p. 64b.

with his *Elvish Queene*. The paradox of superstitious veneration of Homer and Virgil combined with enthusiastic certainty that they may be—nay, have been—surpassed is hard to understand in the twentieth century. The best key to it for us is, perhaps, in Benvenuto Cellini's delight in recording his patrons' praise of his work whenever they happened to say that nothing equal to it could be found even among the ancients.

Ronsard's *Franciade* also appeared too late to affect the structure of *The Faerie Queene*, although Spenser may have watched its publication with lively interest. Its influence upon him, it may be presumed, would have been rather narrowly "classical," for—as Brunetière points out[36]—"si, dans la première 'Préface' de sa *Franciade*, Ronsard s'éxcuse'd'avoir patronné son oeuvre plutôt sur la naïve facilité d'Homère que sur la curieuse diligence de Virgile, ... dans sa seconde 'Préface' ... le nom d'Homère est à peine prononcé, tandis qu'au contraire tous les exemples dont il s'autorise ... sont tirés de Virgile." We do not know what Spenser thought of Ronsard for turning from his Homeric enthusiasm to the creed of Julius Caesar Scaliger. To some of their contemporaries it seemed like pitiable treachery. "Thou souleblind Scaliger," wrote Chapman in 1598,[37] "never didst thou more palpably damn thy drossy spirit .... then in thy sencelesse reprehensions of Homer, whose spirit flew as much above thy groveling capacitie as heaven moves above Barathrum." There is an epitome of all that was involved in Ronsard's declaration in favor of Virgil rather than of Homer in the contrast

---
[36] "*L'Evolution des Genres*," pp. 52–53.
[37] In "A Defence of Homer," *Elizabethan Critical Essays*, II: 301.

between Chapman's justification of the license of his "fourteeners" in his *Iliad* and Bacon's tribute to Virgil. Chapman rejoiced that Homer wrote "from a free fury, an absolute full soul," while the *Aeneid* was produced out "of a courtly, laborious and altogether imitatory spirit."[38] To Bacon, Virgil was "the chastest poet and the royalest . . . . that to the memory of man is known."[39] Throughout their triumphant middle years, Ronsard and the group of poets whose standard-bearer he was, made their Hellenism a charter of almost unrestrained poetical liberty. Du Bellay scrapped the theories of *La Défense et Illustration de la Langue françoise* and told his readers in the *Regrets* that he had learned simply to look into his heart and write:

> Je me contenteray de simplement escrire
> Ce que la passion seulement me fait dire,
> Sans rechercher ailleurs plus graves arguments.[40]

"C'était," writes Chanard (*ibid.*), "l'entier rénoncement aux rêves d'autrefois, l'oubli voulu des prescriptions de la *Défense*, l'abandon de la poésie savante: mais c'était aussi la découverte de la poésie personelle et sincère:

> 'J'escry naïvement tout ce qu'au coeur me touche'.

s'écriait du Bellay. A lui seul ce vers est une poétique."

In the *Regrets* Chanard sees Du Bellay's best work, and in this revival of Leonardo's defiance of the doctrine of imitation—"chi rinunzia alla dignità dello spirito"—we may see a critical movement in the sixteenth century as far-reaching in its results as that doctrine of imitation whose traces are much more

---
[38] Quoted by G. A. Thompson, *Elizabethan Criticism of Poetry*, p. 74.
[39] Quoted by Mackail, *Virgil*, p. 139.
[40] Sonnet iv, quoted by Chanard, *Joachim du Bellay*, p. 363.

susceptible of scholarly investigation. To it we owe Ronsard's prolixity and perhaps much of the prolixity of Spenser. It illuminates Sidney's definition of poetry in the *Defence of Poesy* as an ἐνθυσιασμός, "a divine gift and no human skill." It would seem from the lines which he puts into the mouth of Piers, who is introduced in "October" merely to draw out Cuddie, that Spenser in his youth was a convert to this gospel:

> O pierlesse Poesye, where is then thy place?
> If nor in princes pallace thou doe sitt,
> (And yet is princes pallace the most fitt)
> Ne brest of baser birth doth thee embrace.
> Then make thee winges of thine aspyring wit,
> And, whence thou camst, flye backe to heaven apace.
> —ll. 79–84.

In the following stanzas Piers exclaims that youth, love, and wine are the fountains of poetry, and poetry becomes the sheer outpouring of the inventive impulses of the poet.

Spenser, who was almost indiscriminately hospitable to all literary influences, could combine the Homeric-Platonic with the Scaligerian conception of poetry. He could write "out of an absolute free furie" and yet avail himself of his imitative enthusiasm for unnumbered critical ideas and poetic models. He could pillage the classics of words, images, incidents, and of all the stuff of poetry without being in the least obliged to reproduce their spirit or their form. With Emerson, he was ruler of the spheres and a reverent robber of the brain of Plato and of the art of Virgil.

Spenser's apparent inconsistency went even further. He could accept the principles of Ronsard's later "Prefaces" to the *Franciade;* diverge from them in practice so widely as to seem to have forgotten them altogether; and still regard the conception of epic form which was derived from the *Aeneid* as the basis of his poem and, in a real, if limited way, actually make it the basis of his structure.

It has not been remarked in connection with the form of *The Faerie Queene* that Ronsard, in his *Discours à Très-Illustre et Très-Vertueuse princesse, Elizabeth, Royne d'Angleterre,* sketched the Arthurian legend as the basis of English glory and suggested an epic poem in honor of Arthur (*Oeuvres,* III: 246-47). He made Arthur a pattern of virtue and magnanimity. If Spenser was familiar with *Le Bocage Royal,* he must have seen in it a challenge and perhaps also a revelation. There is no proof that he was acquainted with it and derived from it his unifying figure of Arthur, but Pienaar has suggested (in "Edmund Spenser and Jan van der Noot") that through the Dutch poet Van der Noot he kept abreast of Ronsard's work. Even before he left Cambridge, it seems possible that through Van der Noot's *Olympiados*—which explicitly discussed Ronsard's epic theories in its "Preface"—he may have been attracted by the early "Prefaces" of the *Franciade.* For Ronsard, "the basic idea of the epic should be some incident taken from old annals which has gained credit, like the tradition of Aeneas' voyage used by Virgil."[41] To Spenser, as Mr. Draper has shown (*op. cit.,* pp. 319-20), the Arthurian legends seemed essentially historical. Mr. Draper even points to a passage in Camden's *Britannia* (ed. of 1789, I: 59) as perhaps the suggestion which determined Spenser to "pitch upon Arthur as his super-hero." Camden wrote:

---

[41] *Vide* Storer, *Virgil and Ronsard,* p. 10.

The subject of King Arthur was certainly worthy of the genius of some learned man, who by celebrating such a prince would have immortalized his own fame. It seems to have been the greatest misfortune of this gallant defender of the British empire that he could find no panegyrist for his virtues.

Both Camden and Ronsard may have played a part in Spenser's determination to make Arthur his hero-in-chief, but the discovery of that fact ought not to make us forget that the Arthurian romances themselves—with *Arthur of Little Britain,* as Mr. Greenlaw has remarked (*Britomart at the House of Busirane*), prominent among them even as a structural model—were both the ultimate as well as an immediate influence upon his choice of the keystone for his heroic arch.

There is in *The Faerie Queene* a unifying principle less obvious than the character of Arthur. It is the device found in the second canto of Book II where Spenser translates the lines with which the First Book of the *Aeneid* ends:

> .... intentique ora tenebant.
> Inde toro pater Aeneas sic orsus ab alto.

Medina is entertaining Guyon at a banquet and

> She Guyon deare besought of curtesie,
> To tell from whence he came through jeopardy,
> And whether now on new adventure bownd:
> Who with bold grace and comely gravity,
> Drawing to him the eies of all arownd,
> From lofty siege began these words aloud to sownd.
> —II, ii, 39.

The words which Guyon sounded are an account of that annual banquet held by Gloriana which is the point of radiation for all the adventures in *The Faerie*

Queene. Spenser seems to have made use of Virgil's structural device with Virgil's structural intention. Like Virgil, he plunged *in medias res* in his First Book, but in that book he invented no situation which permitted him to explain the beginning of his action. In the Second Book he made use of Virgil's device of a narrative at a banquet to explain his fable and stressed the debt to Virgil by actually echoing his language. The significance of this is hard to assess. Spenser seems to have been fumbling toward classical unity of plot, but it is not quite certain that he was doing so. He gave an adequate account of the origin of Guyon's quest at a point in his action which corresponds closely with the point in the *Aeneid* at which Aeneas begins his story. Guyon has no story to tell— nothing but a literary device to explain—but the intended analogy with Virgil is all the more marked for that reason.

If Spenser had tried to give similar unity to all of the six "legends" which compose the *Faerie Queene*, beginning them in accordance with the Horatian principle of plunging *in medias res* and drawing the threads together early in the action by a well motivated narrative, we should be sure that he had learned something about structure from Virgil. As it is, we cannot be certain that this story of Guyon at the banquet is not a mere specimen of Virgilian ornament which Spenser happened to appropriate. In the poet's thought it may have had no more structural significance than the legend of Aeneas which Paridel tells at Malbecco's table in Book IV. Digressions into explanatory narrative are of the essence of romance and they sometimes have an architectural value. In *Arthur of Little Britain*, which he regards as "the greatest single influence to be traced in *The Faerie Queene*," Mr. Greenlaw (*op. cit.*, p. 124) remarks not only that the story "is motivated, like Spenser's poem, by a vision of a fairy queen with whom the hero falls in love,—the romance containing the adventures incidental to his search,—but also that the hero tells the vision, after the story is well under way, to his friend Governar precisely as Spenser's Arthur tells Guyon of his vision and his search."

III

Virgil's World in Spenser's Imagination

In his Fourth Book Spenser again makes use of the device of a tale within the main story and again the setting is a banquet with a clear reminiscence of the *Aeneid*. Structurally, the device this time is unimportant, but imaginatively, it makes the "lond of Faery" border close upon the frontier of that legendary Italy where Aeneas fought with Turnus.

Paridel, Britomart, and Satyrane are the guests of Malbecco and Helenore. Their meal is over and a courtly conversation follows. Paridel happens to say that he is "by kin descended" from a grandson of Paris and Oenone, and he mentions the dramatic escape of his ancestors from Troy.

> Whenas the noble Britomart heard tell
> Of Trojan warres and Priams citie sackt,
> The ruefull story of Sir Paridell,
> She was empassiond at that piteous act,
> With zelous envy of Greekes cruell fact
> Against that nation, from whose race of old
> She heard that she was lineally extract:
> For noble Britons sprong of Trojans bold,
> And Troynovant was built of old Troyes ashes cold.
> —III, ix, 38.

Britomart asks at once,

> What to Aeneas fell; sith that men sayne
> He was not in the cities wofull fyre
> Consum'd, but did him selfe to safety retyre.
> —III, ix, 40.

Her answer is the story of Aeneas and his adventures in Italy.

> "Anchyses sonne, begott of Venus fayre,"
> Said he, "out of the flames for safegard fled,
> And with a remnant did to sea repayre,
> Where he through fatall errour long was led
> Full many yeares, and weetlesse wandered
> From shore to shore, emongst the Lybick sandes,
> Ere rest he fownd. Much there he suffered,
> And many perilles past in forreine landes,
> To save his people sad from victours vengefull handes.
>
> "At last in Latium he did arryve,
> Where he with cruell warre was entertaind
> Of th'inland folke, which sought him backe to drive,
> Till he with old Latinus was constraind
> To contract wedlock; (so the Fates ordaind;)
> Wedlocke contract in blood, and eke in blood
> Accomplished, that many deare complaind;
> The rivall slaine, the victour, through the flood
> Escaped hardly, hardly praisd his wedlock good.
>
> "Yet after all, he victour did survive,
> And with Latinus did the kingdom part.
> But after, when both nations gan to strive,
> Into their names the title to convart,
> His sonne Iulus did from thence depart
> With all the warlike youth of Trojans bloud,
> And in Long Alba plast his throne apart,
> Where faire it flourished, and long time stoud,
> Till Romulus, renewing it, to Rome remoud."
> —III, ix, 41–43.

In these stanzas there are unmistakable reminiscences of the *Aeneid*. Upton pointed out that the expression, "entertained with warre," translates Virgil's "crudeli Marte receptus." In

> Wedlocke contract in bloud, and eke in bloud
> Accomplished,

he noted an echo of the goddess' threat in *Aeneid*, VII, 318:

> Sanguine Troiano et Rutulo dotabere, Virgo.

In Spenser's use of "remnant" in the line,

> And with a remnant did to sea repayre,

he might have added that there is an obvious recollection of the Virgilian cliché, "reliquiae Danaum." The bracketed phrase, "So the Fates ordaind," recalls the master conception in Virgil's tale. Aeneas is "fato profugus." Spenser does not stress his translation of the words and the point would be strained by a suggestion that he was deliberately referring to the moral importance of the fact that in the *Aeneid* the hero is fate-driven.

In spite of their echoes of Virgil, these stanzas do not ring as if they had been forged from the metal of the *Aeneid*. Unless it is included in the "fatall errour" through which Aeneas is said to have been led "full many yeares," Spenser's stanzas quite suppress the story of Dido. They add the survey of Roman history from the foundation of Alba Longa by Iulus to the foundation of Rome by Romulus. In the *Aeneid* these facts about Alba and the foundation of Rome have no part in the central story, but they do creep into it in fragmentary prophecies which might have furnished Spenser with all the facts that he mentions and which may easily have suggested to him his allusive, almost apocalyptic language. Three such prophecies are outstanding: the reference in the invocation to the Latin race,

> Albanique patres atque altae moenia Romae,
> —I, 7.

Anchises' review of the future of Rome (VI, 752, *seq.*), and the table of Roman history wrought upon Aeneas' shield by Vulcan (VIII, 628, *seq.*). There is a rough resemblance between the final stanza in Paridel's story and Jove's pledge to Venus of the coming glory of Rome:

> At puer Ascanius, cui nunc cognomen Iulo
> Additur—Ilus erat, dum res stetit Ilia regno—
> Triginta magnos volvendis mensibus orbis
> Imperio explebit, regnumque ab sede Lavini
> Transferet, et longam multa vi muniet Albam.
> Hic iam ter centum totos regnabitur annos
> Gente sub Hectorea, donec regina sacerdos
> Marte gravis geminam partu dabit Ilia prolem.
> Inde lupae fulvo nutricis tegmine laetus
> Romulus excipiet gentem, et Mavortia condet
> Moenia Romanosque suo de nomine dicet.
> —I, 267–77.

Spenser's passage agrees with this in Iulus' migration to Alba Longa and in the founding of Rome by Romulus. His omission of the Dido episode may have been due to the allegorical interpretation of the *Aeneid* which represented Dido as a mere Circe, set to tempt Aeneas from his heaven-appointed way; but it was probably due to his desire to relate the legend of Rome's Trojan origin to the tradition that the Trojan Brutus established the British kingdom. In the later Middle Ages Dido was the saint of Cupid which Chaucer made her in the *Legend of Good Women*—a character which she owed ultimately to the writer of the twelfth-century *Romans d'Enéas*—but the historical and moral predilections of the Renaissance were drawn into sympathy with Aeneas. Caxton's *Eneydos* is a link between the two points of view. It falls into two parts, the first of which contains all the important medieval embroideries upon the Dido story, while the second is a prodigious account of Aeneas' struggle for the possession of Italy. The contest is not represented primarily as an heroic battle between Aeneas and Turnus, but it is conceived as a romantic and very bloody pursuit of Lavinia. The naïveté of the narrative is reflected in the conclusion after the death of Turnus that, "And thus was conquered all Lombardye and the pucelle Lauyne by the hande of eneas." (Caxton's *Eneydos*, p. 162.) Finally, instead of leaving the story where Virgil did, the *Eneydos* added three chapters about the later career of Aeneas and of the Alban kings who followed him.

Miss Harper, in her study of Spenser's use of his sources in the cantos of *The Faerie Queene* (III, iii and II, x) in which the chronicle history of Britain is unrolled in prophecy (*Sources*, p. 179), found reason to think that he worked with his historical material on some critical principle, either scientific or patriotic, which made him select his facts carefully, now from one chronicler and now from another. Among his sources she mentioned the *Brut Tysilio*, Geoffrey of Monmouth's *Historia Regum Britanniae*, Layamon's *Brut*, and Matthew Paris' *Chronica Majora*. If he used these sources in his "chronicles of Briton kings," he can hardly have avoided their influence in Paridel's story, where his real interest in the legend of a Trojan's conquest of Italy was its supposed relation with the tradition of the conquest and naming of Britain by that other Trojan exile, Brutus. He leaves us in no doubt that his final interest was in Brutus, for Britomart interrupts the story of the founding of a second Troy in Rome to exclaim:

"But a third kingdom yet is to arise
Out of the Trojans scattered ofspring,
That, in all glory and great enterprise,
Both first and second Troy shall dare to equalize.

"It Troynovant is hight, that with the waves
Of wealthy Thamis washed is along.

"The Trojan Brute did first that citie fownd,
And Hygate made the meare thereof by west,
And Overt gate by north: that is the bownd
Toward the land; two rivers bownd the rest.
So huge a scope at first him seemed best,
To be the compasse of his kingdomes seat:
So huge a mind could not in lesser rest,
Ne in small meares containe his glory great,
That Albion had conquered first by warlike feat."
—III, ix, 44–46.

The abrupt transition from the legend of Aeneas to that of Brutus in Spenser's stanzas is analogous to Geoffrey's hasty dispatch of Aeneas' story in his three opening chapters. The seventeenth chapter of Geoffrey's First Book recounts the founding of London as Troynovant, and it may very well have given Spenser the suggestion for his forty-fifth and -sixth stanzas.

In the "chronicle of Briton kings from Brute to Uther's rayne" which was opened to Arthur by Phantastes (II, ix and x), Spenser again betrayed the patriotic bias of his interest in the story of Aeneas. Phantastes, who remembered very well the wars

of King Nine,
Of old Assaracus and Inachus divine,
—II, ix, 56.

represented England as infested by abominable giants

> Until that Brutus, anciently deriv'd
> From roiall stocke of old Assaracs line,
> Driven by fatall error, here arriv'd,
> And them of their unjust possession depriv'd.
> —II, x 9.

Perhaps there is in these lines a reminiscence of the recital in the *Georgics* of the victories of Augustus with the prophecy that,

> Stabunt et Parii lapides, spirantia signa,
> Assarici proles demissaeque ab Iove gentis
> Nomina, Trosque parens, et Troiae Cynthius auctor.
> —III, 34–36.

In the succeeding book (III, x, 12) there seems to be a conscious allusion to the *Aeneid* in the account of Hellenore's elopement with Paridel. She robs her husband's treasury of all that she can carry and

> The rest she fyr'd for sport, or for despight;
> As Hellene, when she saw aloft appeare
> The Trojane flames, and reach to hevens height,
> Did clap her hands, and joyed at that dolefull sight.

Miss Sawtelle has pointed out (*Sources*, p. 60) that the only instance of this story in Greek or Latin literature is Deiphebus' account of the scenes at the fall of Troy in *Aeneid* VI;

> Illa, chorum simulans, euantis orgia circum
> Ducebat Phrygias; flammam media ipsa tenebat
> Ingentem, et summa Danaos ex arce vocabat.
> —VI, 517–19.

The parallel is doubtful, for Spenser may merely have remembered as he wrote some contemporary vulgarization of the Troy story such as *Il Giuditio di Paridi*.

A cui segue il Ratto d'Helena con la tragedia dell' Incendio di Troia. Di Anello Paulilli, secondo l'antiche favola (Napoli, 1566), which Peele translated, in its first part, at least, as *The Arraignment of Paris*.[42] The resemblance between Virgil's lines and Spenser's here is very general and a stage version would have been likely to leave a much more vivid picture of the scene in Spenser's memory than would the passage in the *Aeneid*, vivid though that may be.

During his poetical nonage Spenser saw the grandeur that was Rome in a perspective rather different from that in which he viewed it when he was writing *The Faerie Queene*. A widespread interest in Augustan Rome, as a city and civilization quite apart from its surviving literature, had grown up during the Renaissance and had produced a peculiar poetry of its own. It began in Italy with the literature of romantic piety regretting the vanished Rome of the Golden Age, to which many poets of the *cinquecento* contributed.[43] Petrarch and Boccaccio anticipated it. There are traces of it in a realist as uncompromising as Machiavelli. It was sanctioned by the brother-in-law of Lorenzo the Magnificent, Bernardo Rucellai, in his *De Urbe Roma*, and by Castiglione in his *Rovine di Roma*. In Sannazaro's poetry it finally took the form which interested Spenser. His Latin *Elegies* are the link by which Spenser—through Du Bellay's *Antiquitez de Rome*—is attached to this movement in

---

[42] *Vide* Jeffrey, "Italian and English Pastoral Drama of the Renaissance," *Modern Language Review*, XIX:175.

[43] For a discussion of this literature in Italy *vide* Sainiti, *Iacopo Sannazaro e Joachim du Bellay*, pp. 30–41, and Nolhac, *Pétrarque et l'humanisme*, p. 26.

Italian literature. What little imagination there is in *The Ruines of Time* is of exactly the order of that found in Sannazaro's *Ad Cumnas Cumarum*.

> Hic, ubi Cumeae surgebant inclyta famae
> Moenia, Tyrrheni gloria prima maris;
> Longinquis quo saepe hospes properabat ab oris,
> Visurus tripodas, Delie magne, tuos;
> Et vagus antiquos intrabat navita portus,
> Quaerens Daedaliae conscia signa fugae.
> —Liber II, ix, *Ad Cumnas Cumarum, urbis vetustissimae.*

Three distinct impulses are struggling against one another in these verses; medieval fondness for the tragic ruin of glory, the passion of the Renaissance for the glory which has been made inviolate by time's violation, and the melancholy joy with which poetic souls have always contemplated

> The Courts where Jamshyd gloried and drank deep.

All three impulses are felt at higher power later in the same poem:

> Heu tantum imperium terrisque undisque superbum
> Et ferro et flamma corruit in cineres.
> Quaeque fuit quondam summis Urbs aemula Divis,
> Barbarico potuit subdere colla iugo.
> Orbis praeda fuit, totum quae exhauserat orbem,
> Quaeque Urbis fuerant, nunc habet Orbis opes.
> Caetera tempus edax longis tegit obruta saeclis,
> Ipsaque nunc tumulus mortua Roma sui est.
> Disce hinc, humanis quae sit fiducia rebus:
> Hic tanti cursus tam brevis imperii.

Henri Chamard has marked (*Joachim du Bellay*, p. 290) this passage as the link between the widespread treatment of the motif in Italy and its first appearance in France. Du Bellay's *Antiquitez de Rome* is a landmark in French literature because, as Chamard indicates, it stands first in a tradition which embraces Volney, Chateaubriand, Mme. de Stael, and Lamartine. Spenser's *Ruines of Rome* is so literal a translation of the *Antiquitez* that his appreciation of his original may be questioned, but it succeeds in reproducing Du Bellay's conflicting moods of passive reverie upon the departed glory of Rome and of active desire to recreate that glory by the evocations of poetry. One of Du Bellay's sonnets is built upon some lines in the Sixth Book of the *Aeneid* where Virgil's patriotic passion blazes up as Anchises ends his prophecy of the future of Rome. It is the passage which Sainte-Beuve thought the crowning expression of the theme of patriotism in all Virgil's work.

> Viden', ut geminae stant vertice cristae,
> Et pater ipse suo superum iam signat honore?
> En, huius, nate, auspiciis illa incluta Roma
> Imperium terris, animos aequabit Olympo,
> Septemque una sibi muro circumdabit arces,
> Felix prole virum: qualis Berecyntia mater
> Invehitur curru Phrygias turrita per urbes,
> Laeta deum partu, centum complexa nepotes,
> Omnis caelicolas, omnis supera alta tenentis.
> —VI, 779–87.

On this passage Du Bellay based the sonnet which Spenser translated as the sixth in the *Ruines of Rome*.

> Such as the Berecynthian goddesse bright,
> In her swift charret with high turrets crownde,
> Proud that so manie gods she brought to light,
> Such was this citie in her good daies fownd:
> This citie, more than that great Phrygian mother
> Renown'd for fruite of famous progenie,
> Whose greatnes by the greatnes of none other,

> But by her selfe, her equall match could see:
> Rome onely might to Rome compared bee,
> And onely Rome could make great Rome to tremble:
> So did the gods by heavenly doome decree,
> That other earthlie power should not resemble
> > Her that did match the whole earths puissaunce,
> > And did her courage to the heavens advaunce.

The mood and cadence of this sonnet made a permanent impression upon Spenser and in the Fourth Book of *The Faerie Queene* they reappeared, resuming the dress of an epic simile which they wore in the *Aeneid* (vide *F. Q.* IV, ix, 28).

The Ruines of Time was an official poem dedicated to the memory of several members of the House of Dudley in which Spenser made a very crude application of *il sentimento delle rovine*. Ancient Verulam is incarnated as

> A woman sitting sorrowfullie wailing
> > —1. 9.

on the bank of the Thames near the site of the Roman city outside of St. Albans. The poem is a dramatic monologue. Like the knights in *The Faerie Queene*, Verulam feels a dual national attachment and she merges the heroic past of Britain with that of Rome.

> "O Rome, thy ruine I lament and rue,
> And in thy fall my fatall overthrowe,
> That whilom was, whilst heavens with equall vewe
> Deignd to behold me, and their gifts bestowe,
> The picture of thy pride in pompous showe:
> And of the whole world as thou wast the empresse,
> So I of this small Northerne world was princesse."
> > —ll. 78–84.

"I was that citie which the garland wore
Of Britaines pride, delivered unto me
By Romane victors, which it wonne of yore."
—ll. 36–38.

The poem indulges in several prophetic surveys of ancient history in the manner of Hebrew apocalyptic literature. Medieval delight in the tragic drama of history is mingled with the millenarian faith of Puritanism in a Providence that paved the way for righteousness over the ruins of iniquity.

What nowe is of th'Assyrian Lyonesse,
Of whome no footing now on earth appeares?
What of the Persian Beares outragiousnesse,
Whose memorie is quite worne out with yeares?
Who of the Grecian Libbard now ought heares,
That overran the East with greedie powre,
And left his whelps their kingdomes to devoure?
—ll. 64–70.

In this vein the poem mentions several famous ancient buildings (Trajan's Arch, 1. 551 and the tombs of Mausolus, Lisippus, and Marcellus). They are part of the *décor* of the great historic tragedy of human glory eclipsed. Spenser was hesitating between the attitude of the Middle Ages and that of the Renaissance. *The Ruines of Time* is a compromise between the pleasure felt in tragic stories during the Middle Ages—a sense of edification and solemn joy—and the sentimentality of the French and Italian "ruin literature" which he was imitating.

In *The Visions of the Worlds Vanitie* the theme of Roman greatness and decay degenerates into grotesque moralizing on the sin of pride and the mutability of this world. This attitude toward Roman history can hardly be traced in *The Faerie Queene* because there Spenser was guided by the desire to make Roman splendor enhance British glory. A trace of it survives in a passage like that in Book I, where, outside Lucifera's palace in Canto v, Redcross found

> The antique ruines of the Romanes fall,

Romulus, Tarquin, Lentulus, Scipio, Sylla, Marius, Pompey, and Caesar, in the limbo where pride casts its victims. The *letteratura delle rovine*, which was one of Spenser's greatest boyish enthusiasms, was as full of the Christian sense of the exquisite fitness of pride going before a fall as it was of the regret of the humanists for the grandeur that was Rome. "Comment tant de grandeur a-t-elle pu crouler?" asks Chamard (*Joachim du Bellay*, p. 291), in summing up the ideas in the *Antiquitez de Rome*, "C'est qu'une loi fatale s'oppose à tout excès dans la puissance ou la fortune. Quand on monte trop haut, on devient la victime de la Némésis vengeresse. Rome a renouvelé contre le ciel la tentative des Géants, et les Dieux jaloux l'ont punie."

In Book II, canto x, Spenser scattered several allusions to Roman emperors through his list of British kings. Here, if anywhere, we should expect him to show some respect for fact in his treatment of Roman history. Holinshed[44] could not teach him the art of writing history skeptically, but he might have got a glimmering of it from Camden, whom he seems to have admired. His grasp of the facts of Roman history was weaker, if possible, than the level

---

[44] The passage was transcribed from Hardyng and Holinshed and other native chronicle sources without any attempt to separate fact from legend. Kitchin, in his note on II, x, 54, indicates that the passage has some correspondence with Tacitus, but scouts the idea of a connection.

of scholarship in England might suggest.[45] Certainly he did not share the familiarity with the civilization of the past to which Berni, speaking for all the Italian writers of romance, could lay claim:

> Mihi quidem Ciceronis Demosthenisque tempora multo magis nota videntur quam illa quae fuerunt iam annis sexaginta. (Azzolino, *Mondo Cavalleresco*, p. 117.)

How exact was Spenser's knowledge of the times of Cicero and Virgil we can surmise from his sole archaeological reference to the *Aeneid*. It occurs in his tirade against the Irish mantle as the sheet-anchor of the lawlessness of the kerns in *A View of the Present State of Ireland*. Spenser thought that in Virgil's word *mantelum*[46] he had found an authentic forebear of the Irish cloak, the garment-of-all-work, deprivation of which he believed would speedily reduce the bog-trotters to civility. Erroneously, he traced the word to Virgil's description of the dress of the companions of Arcas and Pallas, assembled for the sacrifice as Aeneas first saw them (*Aeneid*, VIII, 102, seq.). The word *mantelum* does not occur in this passage, nor does any word of equivalent meaning, although Virgil in a true antiquarian spirit gave several details about the dress and manner of the Latins. Spenser's allusion to the non-existent *mantelum*, while

---

[45] "Tudor England," wrote Lee, "fell lamentably behind their French neighbors as scholars. According to Sir Richard Jebb, Richard Bentley, the Greek scholar of the end of the seventeenth and the beginning of the eighteenth century, was the first Englishman who can be classed with the great scholars of the French Renaissance. Sixteenth century English scholars were few and their steps were halting. Nearly all their inspiration came from the energetic humanism of France." (*The French Renaissance in England*, p. 18.)

[46] The passage which Spenser seems to have had in mind was *Aeneid*, I, 702, "tonsisque ferunt mantilia villis." Here *mantilia* means handkerchiefs or napkins. For a discussion of the error and various conjectural corrections of it see Riedner, *Spenser's Belesenheit*, pp. 70–71.

it shows that he had an archaeologist's interest in the *Aeneid*, proves also that his recollection of it was vague and that he had probably long discontinued the habit of reading Virgil. Early in the seventeenth century Samuel Daniel said[47] that he and his contemporaries saw antiquity like a superficial drawing of a region on a map, but knew nothing of its real nature. Spenser's treatment of Roman legend as the gateway to British history, his use of the decay of the Roman Empire as a crowning instance of the transition of the glory of this world, and his blundering reference to the *Aeneid* as an archaeological source in *The Present State of Ireland* are three striking illustrations of Daniel's remark.

[47] Quoted by Legouis and Cazamian, *Histoire de la littérature anglaise*, p. 355.

IV

The Common Characters

Spenser's greatest single debt to Virgil is his story of Glaucé and Britomart in Book III, ii. His source was the *Ciris*. Of its genuineness he can have had no doubt, and it had for him the fascination which it had for thousands of readers all over Renaissance Europe. His legend of the love of Britomart and Artegal was patterned as a whole on that of Bradamante and Rogero, but the *Orlando Furioso* begins its story without the prelude of sentiment and idealism which was indispensable for Spenser. In Virgil's tale of Scylla's passion for Minos there were just the elements which he needed and he telescoped the Latin with the Italian story.

The *Ciris* is a tale of the passion of the King of Crete's daughter for the besieger of her father's capital. The pivot of the epyllion is a scene between Scylla and her nurse, Carme, which is the basis of the pathetic dialogue between Britomart and her nurse, Glaucé, in the second canto of the *Legend of Chastity*. Upton, in his note on stanza 30, indicated that there Spenser's indebtedness to his source reached the point of actual translation from it. The relation between the two passages can be shown best by comparison.

Quam simul Ogygii Phoenicis filia Carme	One night, when she was tost with such unrest,
Surgere sensit anus (sonitum nam fecerat illi	Her aged nourse, whose name was Glaucé hight,
Marmoreo aeratus stridens in limine cardo),	Feeling her leap out of her loathed nest,
Corripit extemplo fessam languore puellam	Betwixt her feeble armes her quickly keight,
Et simul: "O nobis sacrum caput—inquit—alumna,	And downe againe in her warme bed her dight:

Non tibi nequiquam viridis per viscera pallor
Aegrotas tenui suffudit sanguine venas,
Nec levis hanc faciem (neque enim pote) cura subedit.
Haud fallor (quod ut o potius Rhamnusia, fallar).
—ll. 220–28.

Tempore quo fessas mortalia pectore curas,
Quo rapidos etiam requiescunt flumina cursus?
Dic age nunc miserae saltus, quod saepe petenti
Iurabas nihil esse mihi...."
—232–35.

Haec loquitur, mollique ut se nudavit amictu,
Frigidulam iniecta circumdat veste puellam,
Quae prius in tenui steterat succincta crocota.
—250–52.

("Ah! my deare daughter, ah my dearest dread,
What uncouth fit," sayd she, "what evill plight,
Hath thee opprest, and with sad drearyhead
Chaunged thy lively cheare and living made thee dead?
—III, ii, 30.

"The time that mortall men their weary cares
Do lay away, and all wilde beastes do rest,
And every river eke his course forbeares,
Then doth this wicked evill thee infest,
And rive with thousand throbs thy thrilled brest;
Like an huge Aetn' of deepe engulfed gryefe,
Sorrow is heaped in thy hollow chest,
Whence foorth it breakes in sighes and anguish ryfe,
As smoke and sulphure mingled with confused styfe."
—III, ii, 32.

So having sayd, her twixt her armes twaine
Shee streightly straynd, and colled tenderly,
And every trembling joynt and every vaine
She softly felt, and rubbed busily,
To doe the frosen cold away to fly;
And her faire deawy eies with kisses deare
Shee ofte did bathe, and ofte againe did dry;
And ever her importund, not to feare
To let the secret of her hart to her appeare.
—III, ii, 34.

Illa autem: "Quid me—inquit—io
  nutricula, torques?
Quid tantum properas nostros no-
  visse furores?
Non ego consueto mortalibus uror
  amore
Nec mihi notorum deflectunt lum-
  ina vultus,
Nec genitor cordi est; ultro namque
  odimus omnes.
Nil amat hic animus, nutrix, quod
  oportet amari."
—257–62.

The damzell pauzd, and then thus
  fearfully:
"Ah! nurse, what needeth thee to
  eke my paine?
Is not enough that I alone doe dye,
But it must doubled be with death
  of twaine?
For nought for me but death there
  doth remaine."
"O daughter deare," said she, "de-
  speire no whit;
For never sore, but might a salve
  obtaine:
That blinded god, which hath ye
  blindly smit,
Another arrow hath your lovers hart
  to hit."
—III, ii, 35.

"But mine is not," quoth she, "like
  other wownd;
For which no reason can finde rem-
  edy."
"Was never such, but mote the like
  be fownd."
Said she, "and though no reason
  may apply
Salve to your sore, yet love can
  higher stye
Then reasons reach, and oft hath
  wonders donne."
—III, ii, 36.

Here exact correspondence between the two narratives ends, to be resumed after an interval. Scylla is ashamed of loving her father's enemy; Britomart, of loving "a shade." Britomart's talk of reason as the bridle of love has no justification in the *Ciris*. The two plots converge again at Spenser's fortieth stanza.

Ei mihi, ne furor ille tuos incaserit artus,
Ille, Arabae Myrrhae quondam qui cepit ocellos,
Ut scelere infando (quod ne sinat Adrastea)
Laedere utrumque uno studeas errore parentem!
Quod si alio quovis animi iactaris amore
(Nam te iactari non est Amathusia nostri
Tam rudis, ut nullo possim cognoscere signo),
Si concessus amor noto te macerat igne,
Per tibi Dictynae praesentia numina iuro.
Prima deum quae mi dulcem te donat alumnam,
Omnia me potius digna atque indigna laborum
Milia visuram, quam te tam tristibus istis
Sordibus et senio patiar tabescere tali.
—237–49.

"Daughter," said she, "what need ye be dismayd,
Or why make ye such monster of your minde?
Of much more uncouth thing I was affrayd;
Of filthy lust, contrary unto kinde:
But this affection nothing straunge I finde;
For who with reason can you aye reprove,
To love the semblaunt pleasing most your minde,
And yield your heart whence ye cannot remove?
No guilt in you, but in the tyranny of Love.
"Not so th' Arabian Myrrhe did sett her mynd,
Nor so did Biblis spend her pining hart,
But lov'd their native flesh against al kynd,
And to their purpose used wicked art:
Yet playd Pasiphae a more monstrous part,
That lov'd a bul, and learnd a beast to bee:
Such shamefull lusts who loaths not, which depart
From course of nature and of modestee?
Swete Love such lewdnes bands from his faire companee."
—III, ii, 40–41.

Here Spenser departs for the space of five stanza from his book. Then stanzas 45 and 46 show fain parallelism. Lines 251–52 of the *Ciris* (already quoted may explain the lines:

> Her chearefull words much cheard the feeble spright
> Of the sicke virgin, that her downe she layd
> In her warme bed to sleepe, if that she might;
> And the old-woman carefully displayd
> The clothes about her round with busy ayd,
> So that at last a little creeping sleepe
> Surprisd her sence.
> —III, ii, 47.

The two perfunctory lines about the coming of dawn in stanza 48 are an unusual abbreviation of the corresponding passage in the *Ciris*.

Postera lux ubi laeta diem mortalibus egit Et gelida venientem ignem quatiebat ab Oeta, Quem pavidae alternis fugitant optantque puellae (Hesperium vitant, optant ardescere Eoum). Praeceptis paret virgo nutricis et omnes Undique conquirit nubendi sedula causas. —349–54.	Earely the morrow next, before that day His joyous face did to the world revele, They both uprose .... III, ii, 48.

In both poems daybreak is the signal for the maidens to try (unsuccessfully) to carry out the advice of their *confidantes*. Then follows in the *Ciris* an incantation which gave Spenser two stanzas almost literally.

At nutrix, patula componens sulfura testa, Narcissum casiamque herbas incendit olentes Terque novena ligans triplici diversa colore Fila: "Ter in gremium mecum— inquit—despue virgo,	Then, taking thrise three heares from of her head, Them trebly breaded in a threefold lace, And round about the pots mouth bound the thread, And after having whispered a space Certain sad words, with hollow voice and bace,

Despue ter, virgo: numero deus impare gaudet."
Inde agno venerata *Orcum* (furialia sacra,
Sacra nec Idaeis anibus nec cognita Grais),
Pergit, Amyclaeo spargens altaria thallo.
—369–76.

Shee to the virgin sayd, thrise sayd she itt:
"Come, daughter, come, come; spit upon my face,
Spitt thrise upon me, thrise upon me spitt;
Th' uneven nomber for this business is most fitt."

That sayd, her rownd about she from her turnd,
She turned her contrary to the sunne,
Thrise she her turnd contrary, and returnd
All contrary, for she the right did shunne,
And ever what she did was streight undonne.
So thought she to undoe her daughters love:
But love, that is in gentle brest begonne,
No ydle charmes so lightly may remove;
That well can witness, who by triall it does prove.
—III, ii, 50–51.

With this incantation Spenser's reproduction of the *Ciris* ends abruptly. No further trace of the poem's influence appears anywhere in *The Faerie Queene*, yet it had one very important effect upon the story of Britomart. The characterization[48] of Glaucé comes directly from the *Ciris*. She is the typical confidante of the Hellenistic epics and she finds her way into

---

[48] The Pléiade was attracted by the Hellenistic tradition represented by Glaucé. Baïf twice used such incantations as hers in his *Eclogues*; first in the Fifth and again in the Sixteenth. In the latter Pacaut takes her nursling, Perrichon, to the forest and pronounces an incantation to recall her lover, some details of which are identical with those found in Glaucé's charm. Baïf's source, however, is probably Theocritus' Second *Idyl*.

Spenser's poem *via* Virgil from the *Argonautica* of Apollonius of Rhodes. Ultimately, we have Apollonius to thank for the fact that Britomart's companion is less of a lay figure than the Palmer of the "Legend of Temperance." In Britomart's name and character, also, it is a temptation to see a projection of the chaste nymph whose story is fleetingly recalled by Carme's apostrophe of her in the *Ciris:*

> ut quid ego amens
> te erepta, o Britomarti, meae spes una salutis,
> te, Britomarti, diem potui producere uitae?
> atque utinam celeri ne tantum grata Dianae
> uenatus esses uirgo sectata uirorum,
> Gnosia neu Partho contendens spicula cornu
> Dicteas ageres ad gramina nota capellas!
> —ll. 294–300.

Aeneas' visit to the grotto of the Sibyl (*Aeneid*, VI, 55, *seq.*) was the foundation of Ariosto's story of Bradamante's chance entry into Merlin's cave (*Orlando Furioso*, III, 16–59) where she has a vision of her future happiness with Rogero and of the line of Italian rulers who are to be her descendants. Rajna admitted (*Fonti*, p. 138) that Ariosto lost almost all trace of the form and spirit of his original, but insisted that he preserved some resemblance to Virgil in the opening and closing incidents of the prophecy. The latter is a skilful adaptation of Virgil's lines on Marcellus to a recent circumstance in the history of the Este family. In comparison with Ariosto, Spenser shows hardly a mark of his ultimate Virgilian source. Britomart's history is the closest of the greater Spenserian parallels to the *Orlando Furioso* (Dodge, *P. M.*

L. A., XII: 178). Like Bradamante, Britomart visits Merlin's cave, gets assurance of her final union with Artegal, and hears a long prophecy of the kings who are to come after her. Such an *apparatus futuri argumenti*, Scaliger pointed out (*Poetices* Liber III, p. 264), was essential.

Quasi igitur argumentum obtenditur toti fabulae in Heleni vaticinio. In sexto, apud Anchisem, futuri quoque imperij tanquam imago quaedam fuit.

Britomart's experience in the cave owes its setting to the *Furioso* and the substance of its revelation of history to British chronicle sources, but it owes its existence to Virgil.

Upton remarked that Merlin's advice to Britomart recalls the Sibyl's exhortation to Aeneas:

Tu ne cede malis, sed contra audentior ito,	"Most noble virgin, that by fatall lore
Quam tua te Fortuna sinet.	Hast learn'd to love, let no whit thee dismay
—VI, 95–96.	The hard beginne that meetes thee in the dore,
	And with sharpe fits thy tender hart oppresseth sore."
	—III, iii, 21.

Virgil's strenuous ethics were much admired by his critics in the Renaissance. Scaliger pointed out that although the *Aeneid* is full of heavenly intervention and revelation of the future (*Poetices*, Liber III, Cap. xxv)—partly reduced to astrological allegory—men are not bound by *kismet*, but are free to resist evil and accept the alliance of their good genius when it offers. Giraldi Cinthio preached a similar vigorous "Platonism" in his *Dialogo Terzo della Vita Civile*, and thanked heaven that

Virgilio è piu tosto Platonico che Stoico, nella maggior parte del suo divino Poema.

Merlin has the same hard but hopeful wisdom to offer to Glaucé.

> Indeede the Fates are firme,
> And may not shrinck, though all the world do shake:
> Yet ought mens good endeavours them confirme,
> And guyde the heavenly causes to their constant terme.
> —III, iii, 25.

Merlin's final words seem to owe a direct debt to Virgil's Sibyl.

> "But yet the end is not . . . . " There Merlin stayd,
> As overcomen of the spirites powre,
> Or other ghastly spectacle dismayd,
> That secretly he saw, yet note discoure:
> Which suddein fitt and halfe extatick stoure
> When the two fearefull wemen saw, they grew
> Greatly confused in behaveoure:
> At last the fury past, to former hew
> Hee turnd againe, and chearfull looks as earst did shew.
> —III, iii, 50.

Upton's notes on this stanza indicate several verbal reminiscences of Virgil's account of Aeneas' visit to the Sibyl's cave.

"But yet the end is not,"—There Merlin stayd."
This abrupt discourse is not unlike that of the Sibyl, "talia fata, conticuit." Virgil, VI, 54, and so likewise the effect,

> Gelidus Teucris per dura cucurrit
> Ossa tremor.

The close of the stanza likewise seems indicated from Virgil,

"Ut primum cessit furor et rapida ora quierunt."

"At last the fury passed to former hew,
He turnd again and cheerfull looks as earst did sew"

Britomart owes more to Ariosto's Bradamante than to any other of her prototypes, but—like Boiardo's Marfisa (Razzoli, *Fonti*, pp. 79–80)—she is generalized from several sources. Marfisa's accoutrements are certainly those of Turnus, while her spiritual pedigree relates her to Penthesilea and the Amazons of Valerius Flaccus. The Britomart who travels incognito with Redcross, and all whose

> .... delight on deedes of armes is sett,
> To hunt out perilles and adventures hard,
> By sea, by land, whereso they may be mett,
> Onely for honour and for high regard,
> Without respect of richesse or reward,
> —III, ii, 6.

is a true heir of Virgil's Camilla. Bradamante, as Edwards remarks (*Orlando Furioso*, pp. 14–15), "figures in one or two minor Italian romances, and has there the warlike propensities and aptitudes which she displays in the works of Boiardo and Ariosto; but her character and adventures in the *Orlando Innamorato* and *Furioso* explain themselves, and need little or no comment from outside sources." Britomart is not a mere projection of the traditional Bradamante. It is a temptation to see in her some traits of the Camilla "whose name first leaped to Virgil's lips as he spoke to Dante of their Italy in the underworld." (Myers, *Classical Essays*, p. 129.) Spenser remembered Camilla with Dante's admiration and in his roll-call of famous women in the opening stanzas of Canto iv, Book III, he recalled

> . . . . how Camill' hath slaine
> The huge Orsilochus.

In his memory was the vision of Camilla pursuing

> Orsilochum, fugiens magnumque agitata per orbem,
> Eludit gyro interior, sequiturque sequentem;
> Tum validam perque arma viro perque ossa securim,
> Altior exsurgens, oranti et multa precanti
> Congeminat; volnus calido rigat ora cerebro.
> —XI, 694–98.

Camilla, however, made no such contribution to Spenser's Britomart as did the Scylla of the *Ciris*. In spite of all her triumphs in tournaments and pitched fights, Britomart never appears like

> . . . . egregia Camilla,
> Agmen agens equitum et florentis aere catervas.
> —XI, 432–33.

There is no moment in Britomart's career so brilliant as that when

> . . . . Volscorum acie comitante, Camilla
> Occurrit, portisque ab equo regina sub ipsis
> Desiluit, quam tota cohors imitata relictis
> Ad terram defluxit equis.
> —XI, 498–501.

Camilla's story has nothing resembling the adventures of Britomart and they are alike in nothing except the quixotic chivalry common to all the daughters of Penthesilea.

Camilla's forest breeding and her training for the chase have no resemblance to Britomart's education, but they faintly resemble—at least in their circumstances of fantastic melodrama— Belphoebe's forest birth and breeding to the service of Diana. In *Aeneid*

XI, 533-94, Juno tells Camilla's story and describes her in characteristically Virgilian fashion by mentioning her accoutrements. Her father Metabus,

> Utque pedum primis infans vestigia plantis
> Institerat, iaculo palmas armavit acuto,
> Spiculaque ex humero parvae suspendit et arcum.
> Pro crinali auro, pro longae tegmine pallae,
> Tigridis exuviae per dorsum a vertice pendent.
> Tela manu iam tum tenera puerilia torsit,
> Et fundam tereti circum caput egit habena.
> —XI, 573-79.

A connection between this passage and the description of Belphoebe in Book II, Canto iii, is unlikely, but the details of Camilla's weaponry happen to be very like Belphoebe's "sharp bore-speare" and "Golden Baudricke," which "forelay across her snowy breast" (II, iii, 29). Upton and Dodge have both pointed out (*P. M. L. A.*, XII:184–85) that Spenser's model in this elaborate description of Belphoebe was Ariosto's Alcina (*Orlando Furioso*, XIV).

The Virgilian figure whom Belphoebe resembles is not Camilla but Venus. Her sudden advent in Book II, Canto iii, seems like a parody of Venus' appearance to the shipwrecked Aeneas. It may be absurd to compare Braggadocchio's shrewd follower, Trompart, who is traditionally identified with the mischief-making valet of Elizabeth's unpopular suitor, the Duc d'Alençon, to Aeneas. The replies of Aeneas and of Trompart, however, have too much in common for accident.

> Cui mater media sese tulit obvia silva,
> Virginis os habitumque gerens et virginis arma,
> Spartaneae, vel qualis equos Threissa fatigat
> Harpalyce volucremque fuga praevertitur Hebrum.
> Namque humeris de more habilem suspenderat arcum
> Venatrix, dederatque comam diffundere ventis,
> Nuda genu, nodoque sinus collecta fluentis.
> Ac prior, Heus, inquit, iuvenes, monstrate, mearum
> Vidistis si quam hic errantem forte sororum,
> Succinctam pharetra et maculosae tegmine lyncis,
> Aut spumantis apri cursum clamore prementem.
>   Sic Venus; et Veneris contra sic filius orsus:
> Nulla tuarum audita mihi neque visa sororum,
> O—quam te memorem, virgo? namque haud tibi vultus
> Mortalis, nec vox hominem sonat; O, dea, certe.
> —I, 314–28.

When Spenser wrote the dialogue which opens his scene between Belphoebe and Trompart, he seems to have intended Virgil's lines to rise in his readers' memories as a foil for his grotesque situation. Belphoebe asks,

> "Hayle, groome! didst not thou see a bleeding hynde,
> Whose right haunch earst my stedfast arrow strake?
> If thou didst, tell me, that I may her overtake."

> Wherewith reviv'd, this answere forth he threw:
> "O goddesse, (for such I thee take to bee;
> For neither doth thy face terrestriall shew,
> Nor voyce sound mortall) I avow to thee,
> Such wounded beast as that I did not see,
> Sith earst into this forrest wild I came.
> But mote thy goodlyhed forgive it mee,
> To weete which of the gods I shall thee name,
> That unto thee dew worship I may rightly frame."
> —II, iii, 22–23.

The resemblance between the two passages stops with Trompart's parody of Aeneas' reply to his mother. Belphoebe is a composite portrait. In stanza 31 Spenser made her

> Such as Diana by the sandy shore
> Of swift Eurotas, or on Cynthus green.

The simile is a literal translation of Virgil's picture of Dido

> Qualis in Eurotae ripis aut per iuga Cynthi
> Exercet Diana choros. —I, 498–99.

Belphoebe's second appearance in *The Faerie Queene* is in Book III, Canto v, where she finds Timias wounded in the forest and takes him home with her to nurse him back to health. Comparison with the marvelous cure wrought upon Aeneas by Venus during his final struggle with Turnus (*Aeneid*, XII, 412–25) at once suggests itself but there is absolutely no resemblance in detail between the two incidents. Ariosto's account of Angelica's discovery of the wounded Medoro (*Orlando Furioso*, XIX, 22) was the active recollection in Spenser's mind as he wrote this scene. Again in Book IV, Canto viii, the dove which leads Belphoebe to Timias belongs to the great family of beast-guides familiar to folklorists and is only remotely akin to the doves which led Aeneas to the Golden Bough (*Aeneid*, VI, 190–204). Upton suggested that Virgil was Spenser's model here but Miss Crane's recent article ("A Source for Spenser's Timias and Belphoebe") makes it seem almost certain that his source was the Old French romance of *Violette*.

In all of Belphoebe's appearances we have seen that there is something faintly and ambiguously recalling a scene in which Venus figures in the *Aeneid*.

The resemblances to Venus were—it is clear—not intentional and perhaps not even conscious, but they may not have been altogether fortuitous. If for any reason the Virgilian Venus was attached to Spenser's conception of Belphoebe, these strange reminiscences of her would be less mysterious. Now it is just possible that—in an altogether unexpected way—the Virgilian Venus may have hovered on the fringe of his consciousness whenever he brought Belphoebe into his story. The key to the mystery lies, perhaps, in the allegorical interpretation of the *Aeneid* which passed current in the Renaissance.

Tasso, in *Il Messaggiero Dialogo* (of Spenser's acquaintance with which I have no proof), accepts the allegorical interpretation of Virgil given currency by Landini, a famous disciple of the more famous Marsilio Ficino, the Florentine Neo-Platonist. He expounds the *Aeneid* as a revelation of truth to its hero in which his mother has a part equivalent to that of Beatrice in Dante's *Paradiso*.

.... quando Enea .... vede Venere, & è da lei alla vista dell'Idee, e delle Intelligenze inalzato; egli si solleva contemplando sovra l'humanità; .... e quando Venere ad Enea, come Diva, si dimostre, non descrive ne l'habito, ne il corpo suo, ma dice solamente:

> Et pura per noctem in luce refulsit
> Alma parens confessa Dea, qualisque videri
> Caelicolis, & quanta solet.

Percische la luce altro non è, che la contemplazione, che fra le tenebre di questo mondo c'inalza alla contemplazione de gli Dei (p. 4).[49]

---

[49] In the introduction to the Petrarchan *De Secreto Conflictu Curarum* a lady like Boethius' *Philosophia* makes precious revelations to Petrarch, who hails her with "Quam te memorem, virgo: Namque haud tibi vultus mortalis: nec vox hominem sonat." She finally intrusts Petrarch to St. Augustine to be perfected in his vision of truth.

From the time when he wrote *The Shepheardes Calendar* Spenser was accustomed to regard Queen Elizabeth as the incarnation of virtue, and this he explicitly says of her in the stanzas prefixed to the Sixth Book of *The Faerie Queene*. The conception there is Neo-Platonic. Elizabeth is Spenser's heaven-sent messenger from "the sacred noursery of Vertue...."

> Where it in silver bowre does hidden ly
> From view of men, and wicked worldes disdaine;
> Since it at first was by the gods with paine
> Planted in earth, being deriv'd at furst
> From heavenly seedes of bounty soveraine.

No less Neo-Platonic is the root of the conception of Elizabeth in the fourth Eclogue in the *Calendar*, for which Spenser chose as emblems the Virgilian tags: "Quam te memorem, Virgo?" and "O, dea certe!" In all her incarnations in *The Faerie Queene* Elizabeth owes something to the Neo-Platonic fancy which transformed Venus into a kind of Beatrice. In the Sixth Book she is "the patterne.... of Princely Curtesie...."

> In whose pure minde, as in a mirrour sheene,
> It showes, and with her brightnesse doth inflame
> The eyes of all which thereon fixed beene.

In the Fifth Book she is Astraea, the Spirit and epiphany of Justice. In the Third Book, as Belphoebe, she is a revelation of the chastity which

> Eternall God, in his almightie powre,
> To make ensample of his heavenly grace,
> In paradize whylome did plant.
> —III, v, 52.

The divine idea shown more brightly in Belphoebe than it did in any other heroine created by Spenser.

> In her faire eyes two living lamps did flame,
> Kindled above at th'Hevenly Makers light.
> —II, iii, 23.

In Belphoebe's story the allegorical parallel with Elizabeth's career is more distinct than it is with any other heroine except Mercilla. Belphoebe behaves very humanly with Braggadocchio, Trompart, and Timias because, perhaps, her prototype behaved so with d'Alençon and Raleigh. To modern readers of the *Aeneid*, Venus seems as little like a prophetess of Neo-Platonic mysteries in her relation to her son as Belphoebe does in her relation to Timias. Yet in the sixteenth century both Venus and Belphoebe could be accepted as guides through the mazes of the active life to the perfection of the life contemplative. Remembering this fundamental identity in what must have been Spenser's conceptions of Venus and Belphoebe, we may be inclined to find it natural that, like Venus, Belphoebe should have "intendiment of herbs" and succor her protégé with "divine tobacco" or panacea, and that she should appear dramatically dressed like one of Diana's nymphs and be hailed, even by such a shrewd knave as Trompart, in words which recall Virgil's "O, dea certe!"

V

Mythology-made Pageantry and Allegory

Certo, l'ammirazione che noi italiani sentiamo così fervida per Virgilio, deriva dal fatto che egli abbia raccolto e fissato le leggende tradizionali, sino allora sparse e labili, sull'origine della stirpe nostra.

The words are the opening sentence of a recent article by Augusto Garsia ("Virgilio") and they reflect the feeling of contemporary Italy. No Englishman in the twentieth century would express himself in the same way about Spenser, yet the author of *The Faerie Queene*, if he is aware of his contemporary fame, must be puzzled by our ingratitude for his service in making us familiar with the work of Camden and Holinshed. The legendary and medieval history of England is condensed for us in the visions of her progeny granted to Britomart (III, iii) and in the "chronicle of Briton kings from Brute to Uthers rayne" (II, x). Geoffrey's story in the *Historia regum Britaniae* of the foundation of the British realm by the Trojan, Brutus, is the historical cornerstone of Spenser's romance. Arthur learns (II, x, 9) that Brutus is his ancestor and Britomart (III, ix, 44) is at a loss whether to be more happy because

> Troy againe out of her dust was reard,

by the founders of Rome, or because Troynovant (London) is rising in England.

When they planned their poems, Spenser and Virgil were confronted by the same challenge from their material. The magnetic field within which the substance of the *Aeneid* took shape lay between two poles; the historic climax of Virgil's own time in which the Roman Peace was established, and the legendary beginnings of Rome. Once the decision was made to base his epic upon the national legends, remarks Mackail (*Virgil*, p. 79), Virgil "definitely rejected two plans; that on the one hand of a chronicle poem on the lines followed by his Latin predecessors; that on the other hand which he had been urged to take both by court-pressure and by the prevalent fashion, of a poem the main scenes and action of which should be contemporary." Spenser in planning *The Faerie Queene*, included both the plans which Virgil rejected. He admitted British chronicle history and its encrusting legends together with all the mythological lore of the classical epics and of medieval romance. Artegal—following the example of Mandricardo, who wore Hector's panoply in the *Orlando Furioso* (XXIII, 78)—is equipped with armor which is

> round about yfretted all with gold,
> In which there written was, with cyphres old,
> *Achilles armes, which Arthegall did win.*
> —III, ii, 25.

Yet Artegal is "son of Gorlois and brother of Cador, Cornish king" (III, iii, 27). His companion-in-arms, Sir Calidore, has as squire, Tristram, "the onely heire of good King Meliogras" (VI, ii, 28). *The Faerie Queene* abounds in legends which cluster around the national hero, Arthur, but which are also brought into contact with the living world of the sixteenth century by means of an allegory both political and moral. Contemporary affairs and contemporary theories of conduct left their trace everywhere in Spenser's web of myth and legend. In the *Aeneid* they left no obvious trace except in the closing passage of Anchises conversation with Aeneas in the underworld.

The wonder is that with his fondness for mythopoeia, Spenser learned so little about the use of national legends and racial myths from Virgil. In his unmapped world the pageant-marriage of the Thames with the Medway and the courtship of the Molanna by the Franchion are the closest equivalents for Virgil's dramatic tradition of the burial of Misenus, whence

> Monte sub aerio, qui nunc Misenus ab illo
> Dicitur, aeternumque tenet per saecula nomen.
> —VI, 233–34

Virgil's sense of the national past was of an altogether different order from Spenser's. It invested every cliff and promontory of Italy with memories of legends like that of the tragic loss and heaven-ordained burial of Palinurus.

> Aeternumque locus Palinuri nomen habebit.
> —VI, 381.

Virgil's feeling for topography was more personal than Spenser's. When Father Tiber reveals the future to Aeneas in a dream, he is a vital presence, not one of the fanciful personifications of Spenser's river-myths.

The amount of purely decorative, Alexandrian myth in the *Aeneid* is small. Full though *The Faerie Queene* be of gorgeous legends, its debts in that kind to Virgil can be very briefly itemized. Miss Sawtelle believes (*Sources*, p. 50) that Spenser's Dryope is Virgilian and that his "aged Ocean" and "Tethys" were an echo of the names in the *Georgics:*

> Oceano libemus, ait, simul ipsa precatur
> Oceanumque patrem rerum, Nymphasque sorores.
> —IV, 381–82.

Of the fifty Nereids whose names close Spenser's canto (IV, xi), less than a dozen have Virgilian counterparts.

Spenser's only reproduction of a Virgilian legend as an unbroken whole is Redcross's adventure with the tree that bleeds and speaks to him with a human voice. Here, however, he was following Ariosto's account of Rogero's adventure with the laurel tree, which proves to be Astolpho metamorphosed by Alcina (*Orlando Furioso*, VI, 28–29), and the correspondence between the English and the Italian is closer than that between the English and the Latin. Spenser tells the story almost as briefly as does Virgil:

> Therewith a piteous yelling voice was heard,
> Crying, "O spare with guilty hands to teare
> My tender sides in this rough rynd embard;
> But fly, ah! fly far hence away, for feare
> Least to you hap that happened to me heare,
> And to this wretched lady, my deare love;
> O too deare love, love bought with death too deare!"
> Astond, he stood, and up his heare did hove,
> And with that suddein horror could no member move.
>
> At last, whenas the dreadfull passion
> Was overpast, and manhood well awake,
> Yet musing at the straunge occasion,
> And doubting much his sence, he thus bespake:
> "What voice of damned ghost from Limbo lake,
> Or guilefull spright wandring in empty aire,
> Both which fraile men doe oftentimes mistake,
> Sends to my doubtful eares these speaches rare,
> And ruefull plaints, me bidding guiltlesse blood to spare?"
> —I, ii, 31–32.

Comparison with Virgil shows several points of identity which Ariosto's version of the story does not explain.

Nam, quae prima solo ruptis radicibus arbos
Vellitur, huic atro liquuntur sanguine guttae
Et terram tabo maculant. Mihi frigidus horror
Membra quatit, gelidusque coit formidine sanguis.
Rursus et alterius lentum convellere vimen
Insequor et caussas penitus temptare latentis:
Ater et alterius sequitur de cortice sanguis.
Multa movens animo Nymphas venerabar agrestis
Gravidumque patrem, Geticis qui praesidet arvis,
Rite secundarent visus omenque levarent.
Tertia sed postquam maiore hastilia nisu
Adgredior genibusque adversae obluctor arenae—
Eloquar, an sileam?—gemitus lacrimabilis imo
Auditur tumulo, et vox reddita fertur ad auris:
Quid miserum, Aenea, laceras? iam parce sepulto;
Parce pias scelerare manus.
—III, 27–42

Virgil's phrases, "parce pias scelerare manus" and "mihi frigidus horror," have no counterpart in the Italian and they are clearly reflected in the English. Rajna has pointed out (*Fonti*, pp. 169–170) that Ariosto took the incident from the *Filocolo* of Boccaccio and that possibly there were other intermediaries between him and Virgil. In the *Orlando Furioso* it is treated as a marvelous metamorphosis which, while it points no moral, yet adorns the tale. Spenser reinvested it with Virgil's atmosphere of moral earnestness. We may suppose that Ariosto's example was responsible for the appearance of the story at all in *The Faerie Queene*, and we can see that his treatment of it was vividly in Spenser's memory as he wrote, but we may surmise that Spenser was haunted by boyhood recollections of Aeneas' shocking discovery of the murdered Polydorus. Virgil's commentary on the story,

> . . . . Quid non mortalia pectora cogis,
> Auri sacra fames?
> —III, 56–57

gave him his invocation to the final canto in Book V:

> O sacred hunger of ambitious mindes,
> And impotent desire of men to raine,
> Whom neither dread of God, that devils bindes,
> Nor lawes of men, that common weales containe,
> Nor bands of nature, that wilde beasts restraine,
> Can keepe from outrage and from doing wrong,
> Where they may hope a kingdome to obtaine.

The fanciful classic myths become even more fabulous in *The Faerie Queene*. Spenser twice introduced protean monsters (III, viii, 39–41, and V, ix, 16–17), about whose versatility he was more explicit than Virgil was about the old man whom Aristaeus seized.

> Ille suae contra non immemor artis
> Omnia transformat sese in miracula rerum,
> Ignemque, horribilemque feram, fluviumque liquentem
> —*Georgics*, IV, 440–42.

In Spenser's amplification of this passage Gough has suggested (*Fifth Book of The Faerie Queene*, p. 17) that we have a compound of Virgilian memories with impressions of Irish outlaws and material derived from English folk tales:

> Into a foxe himselfe he first did tourne;
> But he him hunted like a foxe full fast:
> Then to a bush himselfe he did transforme;
> But he the bush did beat, till that at last
> Into a bird it chaung'd, and from him past,
> Flying from tree to tree, from wand to wand:
> But he then stones at it so long did cast,
> That like a stone it fell upon the land;
> But he then tooke it up, and held fast in his hand.
> —V, ix, 17.

Guyle, whom Talus arrests in this stanza, is a very different conception from the more subtly symbolic Old Man of the Sea whose beneficence Aristaeus extorts.

Spenser's curious story of the Fay who obtained the boon that the soul of her oldest son should pass at death into his second brother, and that the second son's double soul should enter the third brother (*F. Q.*, IV, ii, 52), Upton suggested was an outgrowth of Evander's boast that he had killed a king,

> Nascenti cui tris animas Feronia Mater,
> Horrendum dictu, dederat, terna arma movenda;
> Ter leto sternendus erat; cui tum tamen omnis
> Abstulit haec animas dextra, et totidem exuit armis.
> —VIII, 564–67.

The parallel is striking. If Upton was right in thinking that Spenser here enlarged upon Virgil's suggestion, we can but wonder at its growth into the larger part of an entire canto.

The outstanding mythological passage in the *Aeneid* is the story of Aeneas' quest of his father beyond the grave. Spenser was charmed by Virgil's vision of the *immania regna*, and he drew upon it, altogether, three times in *The Faerie Queene*. Every one of his imitations was inspired directly by the *Aeneid*, yet in every one he failed to understand Virgil's mood of reverent pity for the dead and of curious, speculative faith hardly distinguishable from doubt about the immortality of the soul. Spenser's first imitation of Virgil's hell, if the allegory be taken seriously, should be even more impressive than its original. In his two later imitations he dissolved Virgil's most moving elements into stark allegory.

The first of the three passages is Spenser's description of "Plutoes house" (I, v, 32–36). The Virgilian influence here is certain. Homer's hades in the Eleventh *Odyssey* has no features in common with Spenser's hell except the classic stories of the punishments of Tantalus and Tityus, to which there is a conventional allusion (in I, v, 35). Tasso has no corresponding treatment of the infernal world. Ariosto's story of Astolpho's partial penetration into a hell which is entirely appropriated to inconstant lovers (*Orlando Furioso*, XXXIV) need not be discussed.

Duessa and Night carry the wounded Sansjoy through hades to the haunt of Aesculapius for healing from a fatal wound. They enter "Plutoes house" (I, v, 32) and traversing it, reach Aesculapius' dwelling (I, v, 36). Here Spenser pauses to tell the story of Hippolytus, for whose sake Aesculapius had incurred Jove's banishment from heaven to hell.[50] Sansjoy is healed and Night with her party returns to the upper air. The connection with the Sixth Book of the *Aeneid* is comprised entirely in stanzas 32 to 35:[51]

---

[50] Miss Sawtelle suggests (*Sources*, pp. 64–66), that Spenser's mode of introducing the story of Hippolytus as well as several of his details prove that he wrote with conscious recollection of Virgil's episodic introduction of the story in the muster of Turnus' forces in *Aeneid*, VII, 761–780.

[51] And all the while she [Night] stood upon the ground,
The wakefull dogs did never cease to bay.
—I, v, 30.

The barking of dogs at the approach of day in *Aeneid*, VI, 257, has been indicated as the "source" of Spenser's lines. They belong to a convention of which the following lines from Baïf's Fifth Eclogue are one of many variants:

Flammes du ciel qui suivez la charette
De la nuit brune; o vous bande secrette
Les dieux des bois, o vous nocturnes dieux,
O sous qui sont tous les terrestres lieux,
Tes aspres loix les Tartares escoutent,
Mesmes les chiens te craignent et redoutent,
Quand des enfers sus la terre tu sors.

By that same way the direfull dames doe drive
Their mournefull charett, fild with rusty blood,
And downe to Plutoes house are come bilive:
Which passing through, on every side them stood
The trembling ghosts with sad amazed mood,
Chattring their iron teeth, and staring wide
With stony eies; and all the hellish brood
Of feends infernall flockt on every side,
To gaze on erthly wight, that with the Night durst ride.

They pas the bitter waves of Acheron,
Where many soules sit wailing woefully,
And come to fiery flood of Phlegeton,
Whereas the damned ghosts in torments fry,
And with sharp shrilling shriekes doe bootlesse cry,
Cursing high Jove, the which them thither sent.
The house of endlesse paine is built thereby,
In which ten thousand sorts of punishment
The cursed creatures doe eternally torment.

Before the threshold dreadfull Cerberus
His three deformed heads did lay along,
Curled with thousand adders venemous,
And lilled forth his bloody flaming tong:
At them he gan to reare his bristles strong,
And felly gnarre, untill Dayes enemy
Did him appease; then downe his taile he hong,
And suffered them to passen quietly:
For she in hell and heaven had power equally.

There was Ixion turned on a wheele,
For daring tempt the queene of heaven to sin;
And Sisyphus an huge round stone did reele
Against an hill, ne might from labour lin;
There thristy Tantalus hong by the chin;
And Tityus fed a vultur on his maw;
Typhoeus joynts were stretched on a gin;
Theseus condemned to endlesse slouth by law;
And fifty sisters water in leke vessles draw.
—I, v. 32-35.

The general relation of these stanzas to the so-called Orphic passage in the Sixth Book of the *Aeneid*, particularly in the lines where Virgil describes the punishments of great sinners, is on the surface; but the resemblance between the two passages in some of their details and their contrast in spirit and meaning justify a close comparison.

Lines 4 to 9 of stanza 32 are Spenser's counterpart of Virgil's "inops inhumataque turba":

> Matres atque viri, defunctaque corpora vita
> Magnanimum heroum, pueri innuptaeque puellae,
> Impositique rogis iuvenes ante ora parentum:
> Quam multa in silvis autumni frigore primo
> Lapsa cadunt folia, aut ad terram gurgite ab alto
> Quam multae glomerantur aves, ubi frigidus annus
> Trans pontum fugat et terris immittit apricis.
> Stabant orantes....
> —VI, 306–13.

Spenser's ghosts, "chattring their iron teeth," are a survival of the vivid realization of hell of the Middle Ages. Virgil's lines express the disappointment and universality of death.

The approach to the "house of endless paine" in stanza 33 corresponds to Aeneas' sudden discovery of the near neighborhood of Tartarus:

> Respicit Aeneas subito, et sub rupe sinistra
> Moenia lata videt, triplici circumdata muro,
> Quae rapidus flammis ambit torrentibus amnis,
> Tartareus Phlegethon, torquetque sonantia saxa.
> Porta adversa, ingens, solidoque adamante columnae,
> Vis ut nulla virum, non ipsi excindere bello
> Caelicolae valeant; stat ferrea turris ad auras,

> Tisiphoneque sedens, palla succincta cruenta,
> Vestibulum exsomnis servat noctesque diesque.
> Hinc exaudire gemitus, et saeva sonare
> Verbera; tum stridor ferri, tractaeque catenae.
> —VI, 548–58.

Spenser's "ten thousand sorts of punishment" may be an echo of Virgil's conclusion to his catalogue of the tortures of the damned:

> Non, mihi si linguae centum sint, oraque centum,
> Ferrea vox omnis scelerum comprehendere formas,
> Omnia poenarum percurrere nomina possim.
> —VI, 625–27.

The last verse of stanza 34 may translate Virgil's invocation by the Sibyl of

> .... Hecaten, Caeloque Ereboque potentem.
> —VI, 247.

In Spenser's list of the damned in the stanza following there is much more to contrast than there is to identify with Virgil's corresponding passage. Spenser mentions seven victims of divine justice: Ixion, Tityus, Theseus, Sisyphus, Tantalus, Typhoeus, and the Danaids. Of these, the last four do not appear in Virgil's list. His first two are bare mentions of the names. But his description of

> Theseus condemned to endlesse slouth by law,

is plainly a translation of

> .... sedet aeternumque sedebit
> Infelix Theseus.
> —VI, 617–18.

The details which prove a relation between Virgil's hell and Spenser's are a foil for the contrast between the two in the spirit of their conceptions. Spenser's hell is Dante's inferno atrophied. It is a pale, dying gleam of the tragic, medieval conception of hell as a place where life's seemingly deathless glories are whelmed in a real immortality of pain. On the other hand, writes Glover (*Studies in Virgil*, p. 261):

> Right through Virgil's story, through the mythological, the religious and the philosophical contributions, runs meaning, intention, effort. Every human personality we meet is touched with a sense of the seriousness of being. Life is not extinct at all; the soul is quit of its encumbrances and more in earnest than ever. It is the very antithesis of the Hades of the *Odyssey*.

At the outset of Virgil's passage Spenser failed to perceive the romantic charm of the forest overshadowing the entrance to Avernus. He made the place naked and ugly:

> By that same hole an entraunce, darke and bace,
> With smoke and sulphur hiding all the place,
> Descends to hell.
> —I, v, 31.

This is his equivalent for Virgil's account of Aeneas' approach to Avernus, led by the Sibyl, in the passage made familiar by Bridges—*ibant obscuri* . . . . Spenser regarded the place and its inhabitants with aversion, while Virgil regarded them with pity. "What makes [the Sixth Book of the *Aeneid*]," says Mackail (*Lectures on Poetry*, p. 423), "is the divine Virgilian pity." Spenser forgets the babes, the suicides, and the lovers in the lower world. He gives us only a vague echo of the mythological elements in the *Aeneid*, but his point of view in the passage is no more mature than that of the young Virgil who wrote the *Culex*.

In Book II (vii, 3) Spenser approached hell's mouth again, approached, but passed by and took his champion to the "House of Richesse" instead.

> Betwixt them both was but a little stride,
> That did the house of Richesse from Hellmouth divide.

Again there are unmistakable resemblances to the Sixth Book of the *Aeneid*. Guyon is wandering about and happens to find Mammon.

> At last he came into a gloomy glade,
> Cover'd with boughes and shrubs from heavens light,
> Whereas he sitting found in secret shade
> An uncouth, savage, and uncivile wight.
> —II, vii, 3.

After a parley, Mammon leads Guyon into his "delve." The retreat in a "gloomy glade" is like Virgil's *densis . . . . frondibus antrum*, but Spenser again failed to invent anything like the forest where Aeneas found the golden bough. His grove is another "wandring wood," and Mammon's delve likewise is another "Errours den." After a formal debate about wealth, Guyon and his guide leave the "thick covert" to visit "Plutoes rayne."

> At length they came into a larger space,
> That stretcht it selfe into an ample playne,
> Through which a beaten broad high way did trace,
> That streight did lead to Plutoes griesly rayne;
> By that wayes side there sate infernall Payne,
> And fast beside him sat tumultuous Strife:
> The one in hand an yron whip did strayne,
> The other brandished a bloody knife,
> And both did gnash their teeth, and both did threten life.

> On thother side, in one consort, there sate
> Cruell Revenge, and rancorous Despight,
> Disloyall Treason, and hart-burning Hate;
> But gnawing Gealousy, out of their sight
> Sitting alone, his bitter lips did bight;
> And trembling Feare still to and fro did fly,
> And found no place, wher safe he shroud him might;
> Lamenting Sorrow did in darknes lye;
> And Shame his ugly face did hide from living eye.
>
> And over them sad Horror with grim hew
> Did alwaies sore, beating his yron wings;
> And after him owles and night-ravens flew,
> The hatefull messengers of heavy things,
> Of death and dolor telling sad tidings;
> Whiles sad Celeno, sitting on a clifte,
> A song of bale and bitter sorrow sings,
> That hart of flint a sonder could have rifte:
> Which having ended, after him she flyeth swifte.
> —II, vii, 21–23.

This is Spenser's reproduction of the swarm of human ills which people the approach to Virgil's hell, yet the passages have almost nothing in common. Spenser's "Strife" may reproduce Virgil's *discordia* and the former's "Feare," the latter's *metus*, but Spenser imagined no abstractions which can be confused with those in the following lines:

> Vestibulum ante ipsum primisque in faucibus Orci
> Luctus et ultrices posuere cubilia Curae;
> Pallentesque habitant Morbi, tristisque Senectus,
> Et Metus, et malesuada Fames, ac turpis Egestas,
> Terribiles visu formae, Letumque, Labosque;
> Tum consanguineusque Leti Sopor, et mala mentis
> Gaudia, mortiferumque adverso in limine Bellum,
> Ferreique Eumenidum thalami, et Discordia demens,
> Vipereum crinem vittis innexa cruentis.
> —VI, 273–81.

Spenser's demons haunting the gates of hell are made of the stuff of the medieval Moralities. Virgil's bad angels are the ills to which humanity is heir. The idea of crowding hell's mouth with abstractions came very indirectly to Spenser, but he took a few of his details directly from the *Aeneid*. Celeno (in stanza 23, 1: 6) is taken directly from Virgil's lines:

> Una in praecelsa consedit rupe Celaeno,
> Infelix vates, rumpitque hanc pectore vocem.
> —III, 245-46.

The personifications of human pain which haunt Virgil's hell are supported by a crowd of Harpies, Gorgons, Chimaeras, and Centaurs which in Spenser's abridgement shrink to Celeno, a monster recollected from a quite different part of the *Aeneid*. Virgil's monsters are *somnia*; the real terrors are *Morbi*, *Senectus*, and *tristis Egestas*. In contrast with these realities of experience, Spenser has his moral monsters; Revenge, Despight, Treason, and Gealousy. It was Statius who began to destroy the quality of Virgil's personifications—which, in the *Aeneid*, usually have the vitality of spontaneous figures—by using them excessively and insignificantly. Medieval literature built up the art of allegorizing out of the exhausted classical practice of personifying. Spenser was the heir of both, but he was master only of the medieval art.

Spenser's final reminiscence of Virgil's Sixth Book was a set piece of allegorical pageantry, the description of Ate's house with which he broke ground for the "Legend of Friendship."

> Hard by the gates of hell her dwelling is,
> There whereas all the plagues and harmes abound,
> Which punish wicked men, that walke amisse.
> —IV, i, 20.

Virgil's mysterious realms of death here became an outpost of the Christian retributive hell. His personifications of the ills which haunt the end of life became frankly the plagues meted out to the world's imperial sinners. Spenser was caught for the second time by the lure of the historical pageant of fallen pride with which he closed his great description of Lucifera's court in Book I. His theme was that of Chaucer's Monk, treated in its most grandiose, historical shape. It was the essentially religious theme of Gothic tragedy applied to history, and here faintly supported by Virgil's authority. The "riven walls" of Ate's palace are indistinguishable from Lucifera's dungeon, where her victims

> were by law of that proud tyrannesse,
> Provokt with Wrath, and Envyes false surmise,
> Condemned to that dungeon mercilesse,
> Where they should live in wo, and dye in wretchednesse.
> —I, v, 46.

Among Lucifera's prisoners are Croesus, Antiochus, Nebuchadnezzar, and all

> The antique ruins of the Romanes fall.
> —I, v, 49.

Her identity with Ate is proved by the presence of the same prisoners in Ate's palace outside hell-gate.

> There was the signe of antique Babylon,
> Of fatall Thebes, of Rome that raigned long,
> . . . .
> There also was the name of Nimrod strong,
> Of Alexander, and his princes five,
> Which shar'd to them the spoiles that he had
> got alive.
> —IV, i, 22.

The allegory here and in the myth of Lucifera, Duessa, and Night in Book I is the same. It simply reduces to its lowest terms the Christian doctrine of retribution in the future. The "divine Virgilian pity" assumes a strange guise in these pictures of the gates of hell as a theater for the entertainment of those who took a moralizing or a sentimental pleasure in sad stories of the deaths of kings.

VI

Language and Image

Welcome the *Mantu'an Swan*, *Virgil* the *Wise*,
Whose verse *walks highest*, but not flies.
Who brought green *Poesie* to her perfect Age;
And made that Art which was a *Rage*.
—Cowley's motto to his *Miscellanies*.

Dryden, in the *Essay on Satire* (ed. Ker, II: 28–29), condemned the stories in the "immortal poem called *The Faerie Queene*," but praised Spenser because he "had studied Virgil to as much advantage as Milton had done Homer" (*ibid.*, p. 109). The fruit of Spenser's study of Virgil Dryden summed up with the one word, "fineness." Spenser's verses fired his enthusiasm because they were "so numerous, so various and so harmonious, that only Virgil, whom he professedly imitated, has surpassed him among the Romans; and only Mr. Waller among the English" (*ibid.*, p. 29). To Englishmen in the Restoration the essence of Virgil's poetry was his power to phrase. Dryden praised Tasso for having learned the last refinements of style from Virgil, and commended "the French," who

.... at this day are so fond of them, that they judge them to be the first beauties: *délicat et bien tourné*, are the highest commendations which they bestow on somewhat which they think a masterpiece.

An example of the turn on words, amongst a thousand others, is that in the last Book of Ovid's *Metamorphoses*—

"Heu! quantum scelus est, in viscera, viscera condi!
Congestoque avidum pinguescere corpore corpus;
Alteriusque animantem animantis vivere leto."

Several other illustrations of pathetic but rather jejune plays on words are added, none of which—significantly—is from Virgil, and Dryden's list ends with the admission that, after all, this sort of thing is not precisely Virgilian:

Lastly, a turn, which I cannot say is absolutely on words, for the thought turns with them, is in the fourth *Georgic* of Virgil, where Orpheus is to receive his wife from Hell, on express condition not to look on her until she was come on earth—

"Cum subita incautum dementia cepit amantem;
Ignoscenda quidem, scirent si ignoscere Manes."
—*Essays*, II: 110.

It is true that *The Faerie Queene* abounds in plays on words of the Ovidian kind cited by Dryden. Illustrations swarm:

Meat fit for such a monsters monsterous dyeat.
—V, xii, 31.

"Ah! my deare dread," said then the faithfull mayd,
"Can dread of ought your dreadlesse hart withhold,
That many hath with dread of death dismayd,
And dare even deathes most dreadfull face behold?"
—V, v, 31.

"Against both which that knight wrought knightlesse shame.
For knights and all men this by nature have,
Towards all womankind them kindly to behave."
—VI, ii, 14.

Less un-Virgilian are such phrases as that in the prophecy about the babe, Ruddymane, who was to

Be gotten, not begotten;
—VI, iv, 32.

and that in the story of Artegal's defeat by Radigund:

> So was he overcome, not overcome
> —V, v, 17.

To this Upton saw a parallel in Virgil's question, "Num capti potuere capi?," asked by Juno of the unexterminable Trojans, in *Aeneid*, VII, 295. The meanings in this case are absolutely different, although it is true that both lines exemplify the dramatic antithesis of phrase which Dryden admired. Spenser cultivated this trick of style but whether he caught it primarily from Virgil, and whether it imparted a truly Virgilian quality to his verse, are very different questions. Dryden's own examples suggest a more significant connection with Ovid. Spenser's verbal antitheses in *The Faerie Queene* tend to degenerate into the punning and word-play of euphuism. The style, when it is not deliberately rhetorical, is prone to be un-Latin and ungirt. Crittenden has shown (*Sentence-Structure of Virgil*, p. 40) that "the vast majority of Virgil's sentences are compound." There are only 171 subordinate sentences in the First Book of the *Aeneid*, with corresponding proportions in all the succeeding books. "Detached, simple sentences are comparatively rare." The determinant of Spenser's sentences is the pattern of the stanza and—to a less degree—the scope of the line. His syntax tends to expand its outer limits to the extent of his stanza and to limit its inner rhythms, in spite of frequent enjambement, to the metronome beat of the verse. Many of Spenser's lines are, in effect, detached simple sentences, but most of them are disguised by almost insignificant subordinate conjunctions or by relative pronouns which have a value like that of the Latin relative at the beginning of a period. Formally, his proportion of subordinate sentences is greater than Virgil's; actually, his proportion of simple sentences exceeds Virgil's. As a whole, then, his syntax is not Virgilian, although his style may owe some very definite elements to Latin models.

Spenser's verse and Virgil's both have exceptional smoothness, the quality in the *Aeneid* with which Crittenden is most impressed. Both men habitually wrote "connotative" rather than "apperceptive" sentences, if we may use the terms which Crittenden borrows (*Sentence-Structure*, p. 17) from Wundt. To that extent they are alike. But connotative sentences are a feature of all narrative poetry, and their possession in common by Virgil's verse and Spenser's proves nothing. Compared with Virgil's sentence-structure, that of *The Faerie Queene*, when it is not consciously elaborate, is crudely agglutinative. It escaped the obtuseness of Phaer's translation of the *Aeneid* to the suggestions of its original, but it shows little of the pervading influence of the Latin upon the translator's syntax which Miss Wilcock sees in Surrey's later revisions of his work (*Surrey's Translation*, pp. 144–148).

In contrast with the linguistic Little-Englanders of his century—Ascham, Wilson, and Cheke—Spenser seems foreign in his syntax and vocabulary, but he was not really so.[52] The question is altogether relative. We know, for example, that Ariosto read Virgil all his life with more interest than he did any other poet, yet Croce says (*Ariosto, Shakespeare e Corneille*, p. 23)

---

[52] Miss Pope, in *P. M. L. A.*, XLI: 605, says that Spenser's vocabulary is essentially English, while Renwick remarks, in *M. L. R.*, XVII: 12, that his contemporaries testify by their silence to their belief that it was not offensively foreign.

that in the *Orlando Furioso* he was not a humanist, but a breaker of *il passato* and of *l'arcaismo latino-augusteo* on the procrustean bed of his imagination. J. Shield Nicholson (*Life*, p. 88) says essentially the same thing of Ariosto in language which, however, suggests that he owed a really constitutive debt to Latin as well as to the archaic and dialectal Italian:

> Ariosto adapted some words directly from Latin, he adapted others from dialect, and he gave new and enduring life to words that had gone out of use. He seems to have taken special pleasure in this kind of exhumation, says a recent editor (Papini, p. xiv). Just as Ariosto had a "prodigious aptitude" for gathering materials for the imagination from all sorts of sources, so he had a similar capacity for the acquisition of language.

Nicholson's account of Ariosto's practice can be transferred unchanged to Spenser. It was characteristic of the times. One thing should be obvious about it. It affected poetic diction very much more than it did sentence-structure. Renwick has pointed out (*M. L. R.*, XVII: 1–16) its tremendous effect upon the poetry and the critical theories of Du Bellay and Ronsard, and through them upon Spenser. One marked result with Spenser was—inevitably—the habit of embedding Latinisms in his verse. In his study of *Virgil and Ronsard* (p. 191) Storer summarizes Ronsard's theories of diction in a manner to throw a very unexpected light upon the Latinisms in *The Faerie Queene:*

> Paraphrases are recommended, since Virgil in describing day and night uses "belles circonlocutions" (*Aeneid*, IV, 6–7, 522–25). For spring also Virgil has a beautiful couplet (*Georgics* I: 43–44). For ploughing he writes "vertere terram" (*Georgics*, I: 1–2), for spinning "tolerare colo vitam tenuique Minerva" (*Aeneid*, VIII: 409), for bread "dona

laborata Cereris" (*Aeneid*, VIII: 181), and for wine "Bacchus" (*Georgics*, II: 143). Virgilian expressions for storms and tempests (e.g., *Georgics*, I: 329–33) are worth imitation.

To Spenser's admiration of Ronsard also, quite as much as to the influence of Virgil, we should attribute his echoes of such traditional epic formulae as the line,

> Behold! I see the haven nigh at hand,

with which the last canto of Book I opens, or such as the figure of the weary team with which the transition is made between several cantos (e.g., IV, v, 46 and VI, ix, 1). Similarly Ronsardian is Spenser's language in oaths, although it faithfully repeats some of Virgil's phrases. When Diana refuses to tolerate Venus' search for Cupid among her nymphs she exclaims,

> .... "Goe, dame, goe, seeke your boy
> Where you him lately lefte, in Mars his bed:
>
> .... if I catch him in this company,
> By Stygian lake I vow, whose sad annoy
> The gods doe dread, he dearly shall abye."
> —III, vi, 24.

The annotator may be right in referring Diana's "Stygian lake" to the Sibyl's

> Stygiamque paludem
> Di cuius iurare timent et fallere numen,
> —VI, 323–24.

but the circumstances of Spenser's use of the oath are more like the *hortus siccus* of the French pastorals than they are like the situation in the sixth *Aeneid*. Guyon's pledge—"Now by my head . . . . Much I muse," etc. (II, i, 19) recalled the oath *per caput* to Upton and he felt that in it, as in so many other cases, he saw evidence of Spenser's conscious discipleship of Virgil. In all his Virgilian fragments of phrase, however—in his conventional references to fire as Vulcan and to wine as Bacchus, in his classical epithets for the dawn and the twilight—closely as they may all be echoes of Virgil, we ought probably to see evidence of Spenser's conversion to the taste of Ronsard even more distinctly than we should see in them a proof of his fondness for Virgil. He believed much more emphatically than Virgil ever dreamed of doing that,

> Les excellens poètes nomment peu souvent les choses par leur nom propre. Virgile voulant descrire le iour ou la nuict ne dit point simplement et en paroles nues, Il estoit iour, il estoit nuict: mais par belles circonlocutions.
> —*Oeuvres de Ronsard*, VII: 77.

Behind Ronsard's theories of poetic diction was the doctrine of decorum as applied to language. Tasso stated the principle succinctly in his *Third Discourse of Heroic Poetry*, and indicated its consequences for the epic. "Lo stilo Heroico" he found "in mezo quasi fra la semplice gravità del Tragico, e la fiorita vaghezza del Lirico" (*Discorsi*, p. 25b). Epic poetry should cultivate a calm sublimity. Many are the means to that happy end, but the key to the whole matter is here:

> Sarà sublime l'Elocuzione se le parole sarranno non comuni, ma peregrine, e dall'uso populare lontane.
> —*Ibid.*, p. 26b.

Long before, in *Il Cortegiano*, I, 5. 51–52, Castiglione had stated the doctrine of decorum in epic diction with all its implications for an aristocratic esthetic:

.... se le parole che usa lo scrittore portan seco un poco non dirò di difficultà, ma d'acutezza recondita, e non cosi nota come quelle che si dicono parlando ordinariamente, danno una certa maggior autorità alla scrittura, e fanno che'l lettore va piu ritenuto, e sopra di se, e meglio considera, e si diletta dello ingegno, e dottrina di chi scrive; e col buon giudicio, affaticandosi un poco, gusta quel piacere che s'a nel conseguir le cose difficili.

An immediate consequence drawn from this principle by Castiglione was the remark that the poet must go far afield in search of words fit for poetry. And he proceeded at once to remark that the first to set the good example, by his imitation of the language and style of the Greeks, was Virgil. To learn a double imitation of Virgil, then, was the whole secret of the epic poet's mystery.

To Spenser the word imitation had none of the compromising connotations which it has for us. It meant simply the poet's illimitable draught upon life. Thereby he took possession of the stuff of poetry, of whatever kind, and wherever found. And he felt himself entitled to rifle literature on the same terms that he did direct experience of everything that he found in it, from subject, characters, and situations to "gorgeous words for poetry." It was in the criticism of Chapman's enemy, "soule-blind Scaliger," that imitation first became a limiting principle. In his treatises the change from liberty to law—from the right to rob all poets indiscriminately and inconsistently of whatever in their work fired a rhymer's imagination to the obligation to make the style of one poet the goal of all aspiring—wore the disguise of a master-passion for Virgil. It was that only secondarily. Primarily, it was the first expression of a demand beginning to make itself felt all over Europe for greater lucidity and regularity in literature. Ronsard in his old age and Tasso in his prime were captured by the new movement at its dawn. Dryden formed his opinions and did his work at its noon. Spenser may have had some intimation of what was coming, but certainly he had no such sympathy with the devotees of Virgil as Dryden ascribed to him. He levied his imitative toll indiscriminately and never understood any limitation upon the liberty of a poet.

Yet Spenser may have read Scaliger with interest, even with enthusiasm. His heart may have leaped up to find Scaliger proclaiming Virgil great both in natural science (*Physiologia* and *Astrologia*) and in philosophy (*Theologia*) and quoting (*Poetices*, p. 260) in support of his idea the passage of which it is strange that neither in the Gardens of Adonis nor in *Mutabilitie* did Spenser leave any reminiscence:

> Principio caelum & terras camposque liquentes
> Lucentemque globum Lunae Titaniaque astra
> Spiritus intus alit.

In Scaliger's approval (*ibid.*, p. 264) of the historical prophecies made by Helenus and Anchises there was confirmation for Spenser's own intention to include a chronicle of British kings in *The Faerie Queene*. And in Scaliger's exhaustive classification of the details of Virgil's art it is conceivable that he may have found some stimulus. Scaliger, for example, admired Virgil's skill in his many duels between champions, and he analyzed the technique which gave them their variety and energy. One feature of this is the *exprobatio*, quae fit hoste interempto: de qua inter figuras Sarcasmon enim Graeci vocant. Ea nihilominus ante caedam fiere solet frequens, ut suo loco Neoptolemus,

    .... refers ergo has, & nuncius ibis Pelidae genitori illi mea tristia facta, Degeneremque Neoptolemum narrare memento.

If Spenser read the *Poetices*, there is abundant evidence in the "unknightly railings" (II, vi, 30) which he put into the mouths of many of his champions (e.g., I, v, 11; II, vi, 28; II, viii, 37; IV, i, 44; and IV, iii, 11) that he did not study this passage in vain.

Virgil's "tragical exclamations"—as Webbe called them—were generally admired. Pyrochles' cry to Arthur (II, viii, 52), "Foole!.... use thy fortune," is an echo of Turnus' retort to Aeneas, (XII, 932), "Utere sorte tua." Upton mentioned three adaptations of Turnus' speech in Renaissance literature, the most interesting in the *Arcadia*, where "a young knight disdaining to buy life with yielding, bade [his foe] use his fortune."

The phrase, "past perils well appay," of which Spenser made use in Book IV, ix, 40, to end a recital of hardships, is very inappositely introduced, and is plainly a merely ornamental application of the Virgilian "forsan et haec olim meminisse iuvabit." No Virgilian line was more admired than this by Spenser's contemporaries. Webbe chose Phaer's rendering of it for particular praise (*Elizabethan Critical Essays*, I: 256–57):

First you marke how Virgil always fitteth his matter in hande with wordes agreeable to the same affection which he expresseth; as in his tragicall exclamations, what pathetical speech he frameth? in his comfortable consolations how smoothly the verse runs.

And in the following paragraph Webbe quoted Phaer's rendering of "forsan et haec olim meminisse iuvabit," as a consolation particularly effective in both its Latin and its English dress.

A "tragical exclamation" is again borrowed from Virgil to serve as a pattern for Aldus' cry of grief when Alidine is brought home, seemingly mortally wounded. Aldus exclaims:

> .... "Ah, sory boy!
> Is this the hope that to my hoary haire
> Thou brings? aie me! is this the timely joy,
> Which I expected long, now turnd to sad annoy?"
> —VI, iii, 4.

Riedner has pointed out (*Belesenheit Spensers*, p. 83) that the lines are a paraphrase of Evander's mourning over the body of Pallas:

> Non haec, o Palla, dederas promissa parenti.
> —XI, 152.

In the instances which have just been cited Spenser was more influenced by the poetic theories of his contemporaries than he was by Virgil's poetry. The fragments of Virgilian phrase which he immured in his fabric without regard to its architectural design hardly convince us that he was haunted by the magic of Virgil's verse. They do not indicate even that he shared Montaigne's insight into the capacity of Latin poetry to materialize ideas and to rise to "une puissante conception" (*Essais*, V: 130).

The isolated fragments of Virgil's diction in Spenser's poetry, then, have only the most limited significance for modern readers who may be curious to know to what extent a direct recollection of the *Aeneid* entered into the creative experience of the English poet. In a minor writer such scattered splinters from the *Aeneid* might well indicate a knowledge of it the reverse of intimate or appreciative. The same observation holds of the Virgilian similes in *The Faerie Queene*. Here a general average of resemblance in technique would be more significant than a considerable number of instances where Spenser repeats the substance or even reproduces the phrasing of Virgil's similes. Miss Rowe's testimony (*Spenser's Shorter Similes*, pp. 31–47) that his similes are more like Homer's than Virgil's—if we may trust her critical sense—is better as negative evidence than a score of seemingly directly translated Virgilian similes would be as positive proof of a Virgilian influence upon *The Faerie Queene*. There are, in fact, few Spenserian similes which closely resemble any of those in the *Aeneid*. As good an instance as can be found is the comparison of Maleger's hosts to a flooding stream. They

> .... round about him flocke impetuously,
> Like a great water flood, that, tombling low
> From the high mountaines, threates to overflow
> With suddein fury all the fertile playne,
> And the sad husbandman's long hope doth throw
> Adowne the streame, and all his vowes make vayne,
> Nor bounds nor banks his headlong ruine may
> sustayne.
> —II, xi, 18.

The resemblance here to Virgil's comparison of the Greeks issuing from the Trojan Horse to fire and flood extends to so many details that it cannot be fortuitous:

In segetem veluti cum flamma furentibus austris
Incidit, aut rapidus montano flumine torrens
Sternit agros, sternit sata laeta boumque labores,
Praecipitisque trahit silvas, stupet inscius alto
Accipiens sonitum saxi de vertice pastor.
—II, 304–8.

In his very summary account of the distinction between Spenser's similes and those of Ariosto, Professor Dodge remarked ("Spenser's Imitations," pp. 186–87) that

Ariosto's version [of a typical common simile] is the more precise and effective. Indeed, the qualities of Spenser's style hardly adapted themselves to work requiring point and vivacity. He is more successful, perhaps, in his imitation of Tasso's comparisons, which are rich, one might say Venetian, in effect, and less strictly illustrative.

Mutatis mutandis, this distinction can be applied even more positively to Spenser's similes in comparison with those of Virgil. Spenser's similes are less vitally integrated and less actual than those in the *Aeneid*. There is nothing in *The Faerie Queene* quite to equal the scene where

.... velut immissi diversis partibus ignes
Arentem in silvam et virgulta sonantia lauro:
Aut ubi decursu rapido de montibus altis
Dant sonitum spumosi amnes, et in aequora currunt
Quisque suum populatus iter: non segnius ambo
Aeneas Turnusque ruunt per proelia.
—XII, 521–26.

Virgil used similes with more freedom than did Spenser. The latter's use was confined mainly to the principles of suspense and relief or of simple ornament. In spirit his similes are often nearer akin to the rhetorical comparisons of *Euphues* than they are to those of the *Aeneid*. Although he had no dislike of homely and even ugly allusions, Spenser never followed Virgil in drawing a likeness to a flower broken by the plough (*Aeneid*, IX, 435–40), nor to a boiling pot (VII, 462–66), nor to a "sweated" woman (VIII, 409–13), nor to a countryman treading on a serpent (II, 382–85). It may be asked of Spenser without great injustice, as Augé-Chiquet asks of Baïf (*Baïf*, pp. 218–19):

Ce qu'il admire et aime en Virgile, c'est l'artiste, le génial disciple des Alexandrins. A-t-il vraiment compris ce poète? a-t-il perçu la palpitation etouffée de sa tendresse, été emu de sa pudique mélancholie? On en peut douter. Il reproduit les tableaux virgiliens avec l'application minituese d'un maître hollandais, mais sa peinture est décolorée et sans âme .... Dans la nature, ce qu'il comprend le mieux, c'est le coquet jardin d'Ausone;

A final descriptive tangency of Virgil with Spenser remains to be discussed. Spenser's few naval scenes all resemble Virgilian passages. The voyage in *Colin Clouts Come Home Again*, Riedner has pointed out (*Belesenheit*, p. 71), recalls Virgil's lines:

.... nec iam amplius ullae
Adparent terrae, caelum undique et undique pontus.
—III, 192–93.

Spenser says that the ship

.... Us farre away did beare,
So farre that land, our mother, us did leave,
And naught but sea and heaven to us appeare.
—225–27.

Again, Virgil's description of the Lybian bay that sheltered the weary Trojans seems to have influenced the following stanza from *The Faerie Queene*:

> And now they nigh approched to the sted,
> Where as those mermayds dwelt: it was a still
> And calmy bay, on th'one side sheltered
> With the brode shadow of an hoarie hill,
> On th'other side an high rocke toured still,
> That twixt them both a plesaunt port they made,
> And did like an halfe theatre fulfill:
> There those five sisters had continuall trade,
> And usd to bath themselves in that deceiptfull shade.
> —II, xii, 30.

Virgil makes a far more vivid visual impression, richer in detail, and no less mysteriously glamourous.

> Est in secessu longo locus: insula portum
> Efficit obiectu laterum, quibus omnis ab alto
> Frangitur inque sinus scindit sese unda reductos;
> Hinc atque hinc vastae rupes geminique minantur
> In caelum scopuli, quorum sub vertice late
> Aequora tuta silent; tum silvis scaena coruscis
> Desuper horrentique atrum nemus imminet umbra;
> Fronte sub adversa scopulis pendentibus antrum,
> Intus aquae dulces vivoque sedilia saxo,
> Nympharum domus.
> —I, 159–68

In sum, this analysis of the descriptive elements which Spenser has in common with Virgil shows little significant relationship between them. Spenser's similes and battle descriptions preserve a few petrified traces of the *Aeneid*. His treatment of scenery falls below Virgil's in its *imaginative* insight into landscape. His art in general was too descriptive for particular passages of description to differentiate themselves by their penetration below the forms of things. His conception of poetry rested to a great degree upon a misinterpretation, all but universal in the Renaissance,[53] of the Horatian dictum, *ut pictura poesis*, which encouraged him to allow his amazingly pictorial genius to conceive the entire *Faerie Queene* as a vast tapestry. Poetry became a branch of heroic painting in which Spenser believed that "poets witt .... passeth painter farre" in the use of the "life resembling pencill" (III, introductory stanza ii). In the medium of words the artist's "daedale hand" must achieve effects at once realistic, dramatic, and chryselephantine. The result was Bowers of Bliss and Masques of Cupid amid walls frescoed with the loves of the gods. This is the quintessence of Alexandrianism. It is a major element with Spenser, but an extremely minor one with Virgil. At only one point does it lead to direct intersection of their narratives. From Virgil's picture of Ganymede,

> .... quem praepes ab Ida
> Sublimen pedibus rapuit Iovis armiger uncis;
> Longaevi palmas nequiquam ad sidera tendunt
> Custodes, saevitque canum latratus in auras.
> —V, 254–57.

we can turn with confidence to Spenser's cameo:

> Twise was he seene in soaring eagles shape,
> And with wide winges to beat the buxome ayre:
> Once, when he with Asterie did scape,
> Againe, when as the Trojane boy so fayre
> He snatcht from Ida hill, and with him bare:
> Wondrous delight it was, there to behould
> How the rude shepheardes after him did stare,
> Trembling through feare least down he fallen should,
> And often to him calling to take surer hould.
> —III, xi, 34.

---

[53] "Du mot fameux d'Horace—Ut pictura poesis—que d'ailleurs il comprend à faux—il déduit une conclusion inattendue, 'la poèsie est comme la peincture'," writes Chamard, *Joachim du Bellay*, p. 205.

This appropriation of the decorative motif of the rape of Ganymede is less an evidence of Virgil's influence upon Spenser than it is an example of Spenser's truth to his own self in his eclectic pilfering from all available literary treasuries.

To realize the contrast between the two poets in the descriptive aspects of their work we need only recall the main trend of criticism of each. Lowell's opinion is, probably, final, at least as far as its main proposition goes. We read Spenser not for his allegory but for his sensuous appeal. We read Virgil for the drama and meaning of his story. His development as a poet was steadily away from the Alexandrianism of his early models and of his own youthful work.[54] The growth of the two poets was in opposite directions. Spenser's mature work, as Professor Baskerville has shown ("Genesis of Spenser's Faerie Queene"), seems like the lengthened shadow of the masques in honor of Elizabeth which he saw at Kenilworth and Woodstock while he was still in the service of Leicester.

---

[54] Glover, *Studies in Virgil*, p. 54, remarks that Virgil's development was steadily away from the Alexandrianism of his own early work, such as the *Culex*, and of his Greek models. He contrasts the plainness of the *Aeneid* with the luxuriance of the *Argonautica*. "Apollonius' adornments are pictures—and pretty pictures, Aphrodite combing her hair, Aphrodite breaking Eros' arrows, Eros playing with Ganymede at dice—all these are of the type which Alexandrian painters loved to paint, but they have nothing to do with Jason and Medea. They are a bribe to the reader."

VII

The Admiration of a Profound Philosopher

The Elizabethans were uncertain which to admire more in Virgil, the style that goaded them to the black magic of quantitative hexameters in the effort to recapture its beauty, or the high morality. Stanyhurst, in the Introduction to his translation of the *Aeneid*, expressed the feeling of his contemporaries quite naïvely. After lamenting the critical spirit in which Ennius, Horace, Juvenal, and Persius wrote their "bitter quippes" which made them unsuitable for the reader of serious aspirations, he turned affectionately to "oure Virgil":

But oure Virgil, not content wyth such meigre stuffe, dooth laboure in telling as it were a Canterburye tale, too ferret out thee secretes of Nature, with woordes so fitlye coucht, wyth verses so smoothlye slyckte, with sentences so featlye orderd, with orations so neatlie burhisht, with similitudes so aptly applyed, with eche decorum so duely observed, as in truth hee hath in right purchast to hym self thee name of a surpassing poet, thee fame of an od oratour, and thee admiration of a profound philosopher.
—*Elizabethan Critical Pamphlets*, p. 137.

It is not precisely as a profound philosopher that we admire Virgil today, and the prevailing view of Spenser as a thinker may be stated in Goethe's dictum about Byron; "As soon as he reflects, he is a child." *The Faerie Queene* is frankly a book of hero-worship, and to readers in the twentieth century such a book seems worse than naïve: it seems hypocritical. M. Huizinga has shown (*Waning of the Middle Ages*,

p. 30) that the imitation "of the hero and the sage" is an anti-democratic conception which "bears as a *vitium originis* the stamp of aristocratic exclusiveness" and which is really "a quest of oblivion, sought in the delusion of ideal harmony." Spenser, then, and Virgil too, in so far as Spenser was right in considering him as having in the *Aeneid* "ensaumpled a good governour and a virtuous man," run the almost certain hazard today of being regarded as more or less fundamentally insincere. Both men seem to have been touts for the governing class—mere panders to the egotism and inertia of the idealism of that class. Spenser's delusion that he was writing a "booke" of which the "generall end is . . . . to fashion a gentleman or noble person in vertuous and gentle discipline" had its just reward in his ironical failure as a petitioner for royal favor. Virgil also—in so far as the Renaissance was right in looking at the *Aeneid* as Aeneas Sylvius admonished it to do—got justice in being consigned to the hatred of schoolboys.

Sylvius, in the *De Liberorum Educatione*, echoed the tradition of the Middle Ages as well as the opinion of his own times when he wrote:

> Following ancient precedent, Homer and Virgil, the masters of the heroic style, should be your first choice in poetry. The loftiness of theme and the romantic spirit of the *Iliad* and the *Aeneid* mark them out, as Augustine held, as an inspiring training for boys.

That the *Aeneid*, at least as recently as Dryden's day, was regarded as an inspiring book for men is a fact very hard to comprehend in the twentieth century. We feel a glimmer of sympathy with the reasoning of Sidney's *Apology for Poetry*, but we find it difficult to believe that the author of an essay for its age so enlightened could have said in it that, "No philosopher's precepts can sooner make you an honest man than the reading of Virgil." As Paul Shorey observes ("Literature and Modern Life," p. 618), "to estimate literature by the residuum of knowledge, common sense, and sane habits of thought that it deposits in the mind" seems to most of us "a crude criterion." The criterion may be crude, but the fact, if true, does not excuse us from examining those of its implications which were filaments relating the mind that imagined *The Faerie Queene* to the mind that created the *Aeneid*, as Spenser and his contemporaries understood that mind.

That his contemporaries and he himself misunderstood Virgil must be our point of departure. It was not possible to enjoy Virgil in the sixteenth century without being superstitious about him. Miss Nitchie (*Virgil and the English Poets*, p. 17) has sketched the traditional view of Virgil as an allegorist whose poetry concealed the master mysteries of morality and even of the Christian religion. She indicates it in Fulgentius, Dante (*Convito*), John of Salisbury, and Bernard of Chartres, and remarks that the notion of a hidden meaning was still strong in the Prologues to several of the books of Gavin Douglas's translation of the *Aeneid*, and in Spenser's letter to Raleigh. It was, of course, positively asserted by Scaliger (*Poetices*, Liber III, 25, pp. 265–66), who made it a key to the divine machinery of the poem which he rationalized on an astrological basis, and saw in it an expression of the Socratic doctrine of contending good and evil geniuses. For Scaliger, we learn, Aeneas was the perfected man, and "Hominis perfectio consummetur contemplatione" (Liber III, 10, p. 207). The vagaries into which allegorical interpretation of the *Aeneid* could lead had, indeed, long been illustrated by Petrarch's assertion that Virgil's subject was the perfect man, that in Venus we have an allegory of pleasure, and in the winds and in Aeolus respectively, symbols of the passions and of restraining reason. Petrarch and Scaliger agreed on the essential matter of making the exemplar of Roman endurance and activity a pattern for the Christian ideal of contemplation. Their misinterpretation of Aeneas' interview with Anchises in hell may have had no effect upon Spenser's plan to end his "Legend of Holiness" by conducting his hero to a mountain peak for an interview with an old seer whose name is Contemplation and whose part it is to give the final perfecting to his nature. It is, however, worth remark that the pattern of his First Book corresponds with the very unhistorical moral which they read into the *Aeneid*.

The prince of Virgilian allegorists was Christopher Landini of the Platonic Academy in Florence. There is no proof that Spenser knew his chief work, the *Disputationes Camaldulenses*, but its interpretation of the *Aeneid* makes that poem correspond in all essentials with Spenser's "Legends of Holiness" and "of Temperance." Landini's first book is "De Vita Activa et Contemplativa" and his second is "De Summo Bono." His third and fourth books are a series of "Allegorie in Virgilium" which represent the *Aeneid* as allegorically exemplifying the theories of the other two. Aeneas' visit to the cave of the Sibyl is interpreted in a way which makes it correspond with Redcross's experience with Contemplation. "Antrum immane petit, quod cum facit ad res divinas contemplandas erigitur." Aeneas' experience in the cave is represented as a Platonic vision of truth and through it he achieves the ideal of perfection through contemplation of the supreme good.

> Aeneas divinarum rerum sibi contemplationem finem proposuit .... Nam adventus in Italiam ostendit habitum virtutum iam contractum ita: ut a proposita vita non sit discessurus aeneas.
> —16.

The golden bough is wisdom. The descent to hell is temptation and the diseases at hell's gate are perturbations.

Here Landini's interpretation of the *Aeneid* loses its resemblance to the First Book of *The Faerie Queene* but begins to recall the second. Virgil's monsters about the gates of Dis are described one after another as temptations or perturbations. The embodiments of Virgilian pity become allegories of sin. *Male suada fames* and *turpis egestas* are treated as varieties of *auri sacra fames*. The four rivers of hell become perturbations which test the firmness of Aeneas' virtue. Fortified by the golden bough, he moves among them unharmed, just as Guyon does, accompanied by the Palmer, among the stormy temptations of the "Legend of Temperance." Aeneas' marble temple to Apollo is only a symbol of the fact that, "sic mens nullis perturbationibus frangatur sed illas frangat" (p. 20). The entire *Aeneid*, like Spenser's Second Book, is but an allegory showing that

> Who ever doth to temperaunce apply
> His stedfast life, and all his actions frame,
> Trust me, shall find no greater enimy,
> Than stubborne perturbation, to the same.
> —II, v, 1.

For Landini and Scaliger alike, the final meaning of the *Aeneid* consisted in its union of the principle of resistance to evil as incarnated in Aeneas with that of divine providence as less satisfactorily represented by the interferences of the gods in his story. Scaliger's expression of the latter idea seems to us quaint, if not absurd, but it is worth while to remind ourselves that to Virgil's most authoritative and modern interpreters (Heinze, *Epische Technik*, p. 285, and Prescott, *Virgil's Art*, pp. 250–61) the meaning which Virgil intended his poem to convey to his contemporaries is bound up in his conception of Fate as embodied in the really monotheistic figure of Jove. The other gods are the agents of the divinity who controls the destiny of the wandering Trojans.

In *The Faerie Queene* Spenser combined the principles of resistance to evil and of divine providence conspicuously in his Second Book. Guyon's adventures are an illustration of the paradox which is implicit in the union of those two principles. Like Aeneas, he takes arms against a sea of troubles and, again like Aeneas, he is constantly in need of metaphysical aid. At the crucial moment it is always at hand. As if to leave us in no doubt of his meaning, Spenser put his famous profession of faith in the care of heaven at the turning point in Guyon's story, at the head of the eighth canto of the Second Book.

> And is there care in heaven? And is there love
> In heavenly spirits to these creatures bace,
> That may compassion of their evilles move?
> There is: else much more wretched were the cace
> Of men then beasts. But O th'exceeding grace
> Of highest God that loves his creatures so.

In the allegorical interpretation of the *Aeneid* by the Neo-Platonic writers of the Renaissance we have the key to the allegory of *The Faerie Queene*. The actions suitable to heroic poetry, wrote Tasso (*Opere*, XII, p. 7), are

> Le forme della fortezza, della temperanza, della prùdenza, della fede, e della pietà, e della religione, e d'ogni altra virtù, la quale, o sia acquistata per lunga esercitazione, o infusa per grazia divina.

In Tasso's long exercise and grace divine we have crystallized the essence of the theory which Landini inherited and so amazingly developed in the *Disputationes Camaldulenses*—the theory that Aeneas is made perfect by contemplation of God and that he is disciplined for the mystical experience by the perturbations of the active life. In Tasso's list of heroic virtues we have the real basis of the division of *The Faerie Queene* into "the twelve morall virtues which Aristotle hath devised." Aristotle, of course, was only one in a distinguished galaxy who contributed to the Spenserian virtues. Over them all was flung a veil of mysticism dyed in the colors of the allegorical interpretation which the Renaissance read into Virgil's conception of Aeneas. Even for so unmystical a critic as Sperone, Aeneas possessed "cotale habito di fortezza, o di prudenza, o di temperantia." All these qualities, which "volle Virgilio significare per la presenza di Venere" (*Dialoghi*, p. 284), were for the school of Landini but the discipline preliminary to a spiritual consummation not unlike that to which Beatrice guided Dante, but more like that to which Una guided the Knight of the Red Cross.

The profoundest Virgilian philosophy which could be embodied in *The Faerie Queene* was the Sibyl's wisdom, *Ne cede malis,* but it had been strangely Christianized. The Neo-Platonic commentators made the Sibyl's advice the basis of an ascetic allegory. The epic of Augustan Rome became a parable of the struggle of "the resolved soul with created pleasure." Spenser conceived a romance the whole ethos and plan of which were involved in that struggle. In doing so he may seem today to have written with his intellect and imagination in shackles to medieval tradition. We cannot, however, discount the fact that the vague "philosophy" of moral earnestness which Spenser's contemporaries found in the *Aeneid* penetrated the conception of epic poetry held by all thinking men. The "high seriousness" of *The Faerie Queene* may owe much directly to Virgil. Certainly it owes something to the mystical interpretation of his work by his allegorical commentators. At the opening of the first dialogue of the *Secretum* Saint Augustine quoted the Stoic maxim, *Sic itur ad astra* (*Aeneid,* IX, 641) and Petrarch accepted it as the guide of life, never doubting that Virgil would approve the application of his maxim by the Christian saint. We have seen that Landini in the *Disputationes Camaldulenses* interpreted Virgil's epic as an allegory corresponding fundamentally with Spenser's "Legend of Temperance." Spenser's admiration for Virgil, the "profound philosopher," may have been unhistorical but it was not naïve, and it was quite as important a factor in the creation of *The Faerie Queene* as was his admiration for Virgil, the artist.

BIBLIOGRAPHY

This bibliography is limited to books and articles to which reference is made in the text. The following abbreviations are used:

P. M. L. A.   Publications of the Modern Language Association of America
Mod. Phil.   Modern Philology
J. E. G. P.   Journal of English and Germanic Philology
M. L. R.   Modern Language Review
S. Phil.   Studies in Philology
M. L. N.   Modern Language Notes

AENEAS SYLVIUS.
 De liberorum educatione, translated by William H. Woodward in Vittorino da Feltre and other humanist Educators (Cambridge University Press, 1897).

ARIOSTO, LUDOVICO.
 L'Orlando Furioso, ed. by Augusto Romizi (Milan, 1900).

AUGÉ-CHIQUET, MATHIEU.
 La vie, les idées et l'oeuvre de Jean-Antoine de Baïf (Paris, 1909).

AZZOLINO, ALBERICO DI.
 Il mondo cavalleresco di Boiardo, Ariosto, Berni (Palermo, 1912).

BAÏF, JEAN ANTOINE DE.
 Oeuvres ("La Pléiade française," ed. by C. Marty-Laveux. 1886).

BASKERVILLE, CHARLES READ.
 "Genesis of Spenser's 'Faerie Queene'," Mod. Phil., XVIII: 49-54.

BELLAY, JOACHIM DU.
 La Défense et l'illustration de langue françoise (ed. by C. Marty-Lavaux. Paris, 1886).

BLANCHARD, HAROLD H.
 "Spenser and Boiardo," P. M. L. A., XL: 828-51.

BOCCACCIO, GIOVANNI.
 Il 'Buccolicum carmen' trascritto di su l'autografo Riccardiano e illustrato per cura di Giacomo Lidonnici (Città di Castello, 1914).

BOIARDO, MATTEO.
 Orlando innamorato (Milan, 1806).

BRENNER, EDUARD J. W.
 Phaer's Virgilubersetzung in ihrem Verhaltnis sum Original (Heidelberg, 1912).

BRUNETIÈRE, FERDINAND.
L'évolution des genres dans l'histoire de la littérature (ed. 7; Paris, 1922).

BURTON, ROBERT.
The Anatomy of Melancholy (edited by A. R. Shilleto. London, 1903).

CAMOENS, LUIZ DE
Os Lusiados (Tr. by Sir Richard Burton. London, 1880).

CASTIGLIONE, BALDASSARE.
Il Cortigiano (Vinetia, 1544).

CAXTON, WILLIAM.
Eneydos ("Early English Text Society's Publications," Series 2, No. 57. London, 1890).

CHAMARD, HENRI.
Joachim du Bellay ("Travaux et Mémoires de l'Université de Lille." Tome 8. 1900).

CORY, HERBERT E.
Edmund Spenser, a Critical Study (University of California Press. 1917).

COWLEY, ABRAHAM.
Poems, Miscellanies, The Mistress, Pindarique Odes, Davideis, Verses written on several occasions (ed. by A. R. Waller. Cambridge, 1905).

CRANE, CLARA W.
"A Source for Spenser's Timias and Belphoebe," P. M. L. A., XLIII: 635–44.

CRITTENDEN, ALBERT R.
The Sentence-structure of Virgil (Ann Arbor, 1911).

CROCE, BENEDETTO.
Ariosto, Shakespeare and Corneille (Bari, 1920).

DANTE, ALIGHIERI.
La Divina Commedia (ed. by T. Casini. Firenze, 1909).

DE WITT, NORMAN.
Virgil's Biographia Literaria (Victoria College Press. 1923).

DODGE, RALPH W. N.
Spenser's Imitations from Ariosto, P. M. L. A., XII: 151–204.

DONATUS.
Life of Virgil (Tr. by Thomas Phaer and prefixed to his translation of the Aeneid. 1584).

DRAPER, JOHN W.
"The Narrative Technique of 'The Faerie Queene'," P. M. L. A., XXXIX: 310–24.

DRYDEN, JOHN.
Essays (Selected and edited by W. P. Ker. Oxford, 1900).

EDWARDS, ERNEST W.
  The 'Orlando Furioso' and its Predecessors (Cambridge University Press, 1924).
EMERSON, OLIVER F.
  "Spenser's Virgil's 'Gnat'," *J. E. G. P.*, XVII: 94–118.
ERSKINE, JOHN.
  "The Virtue of Friendship in 'The Faerie Queene'," *P. M. L. A.*, XXX: 831–50.
FLETCHER, JEFFERSON B.
  "Areopagus and Pléiade," *J. E. G. P.*, II: 440–53.
FLETCHER, PHINEAS.
  The Poems of Phineas Fletcher, ed. by Alexander Grosart. (The Fuller Worthies' Library, 1869).
FRANK, TENNEY.
  Virgil, a Biography (New York, 1922).
GARSIA, AUGUSTO.
  "Virgilio," *Il Giornale di Politica e di Letteratura*, VI: 300–6.
GEOFFREY OF MONMOUTH.
  Geoffrey of Monmouth translated by Sebastian Evans (London, 1904).
GREENE, ROBERT, AND PEELE, GEORGE.
  Dramatic and Poetic Works (ed. by A. Dyce. London, 1883).
GLOVER, TERROT R.
  Studies in Virgil (London, 1904).
GREENLAW, EDWIN A.
  "Britomart at the House of Busirane." *S. Phil.*, XXVI, 117–130.
  "Some Old Religious Cults in Spenser," *S. Phil.*, XX: 140–62.
  "Spenser and Lucretius," *S. Phil.*, XVII: 439–64.
  "Spenser's Fairy Mythology," *S. Phil.*, XV: 105–22.
GREG, W. W.
  Pastoral Poetry and Pastoral Drama (London, 1906).
HALL, JOSEPH.
  Satires (edited by Samuel W. Singer; Chiswick, 1824).
HARPER, C. A.
  The Sources of the British Chronicle History in Spenser's 'Faerie Queene' (Philadelphia, 1910).
HEINZE, RICHARD.
  Virgils Epische Technik (Leipzig, 1903).
HIGGINSON, JAMES J.
  Spenser's Shepherd's Calendar in Relation to Contemporary Affairs (New York, 1912).

HUGHES, MERRITT Y.
"*Spenser and the Greek Pastoral Triad,*" *S. Phil.*, XX: 184–215.
HUIZINGA, J.
The Waning of the Middle Ages (London, 1924).
JEBB, SIR RICHARD.
Bentley (New York, 1882).
JEFFREY, V. M.
"*Italian and English Pastoral drama in the Renaissance,*" *M. L. R.*, XIX: 56, 175, 435.
KLUGE, F.
"Spenser's Shepheardes Calendar," *Anglia*, III: 266–74.
KOEPPEL, E.
Englische Tassoübersetzungen, *Anglia*, XI: 333–62.
LANDINI, CRISTOFORO.
Allegorie Platonicae in XII lib. Aeneidos Basileae (Ex. Off. Henriceptrina. 1577).
LANSON, GUSTAVE.
Histoire de la littérature française (Paris, 1909).
LEE, SIR SIDNEY.
The French Renaissance in England (New York, 1910).
LEGOUIS, EMILE H.
Spenser (Paris, 1924).
LEGOUIS, EMILE H., AND CAZAMIAN, LOUIS.
Histoire de la littérature anglaise (Paris, 1924).
LILLY, MARIE LORETTO.
The Georgic (Baltimore, 1919).
MACKAIL, JOHN W.
Lectures on Poetry (London, 1911).
Virgil and his Meaning to the World To-day (Boston, 1922).
MANTOVANO, BATTISTA.
The Eclogues of Baptista Mantuanus (ed. by Wilfred P. Mustard. Johns Hopkins University Press, 1911).
MARLOWE, CHRISTOPHER.
The Tragedy of Dido Queen of Carthage (Tudor Facsimile Text).
MAYNADIER, HAROLD.
"*The Areopagus of Sidney and Spenser,*" *M. L. R.*, IV: 289–301.
MCMURPHY, SUSANNAH J.
Spenser's Use of Ariosto for Allegory (University of Washington Press, 1924).
MENENDEZ Y PELAYO.
Eglogas y Georgicas (ed. by P. Felix M. Hidalgo and Miguel A. Caro).

Montaigne, Michel de.
  Les Essais (La Renaissance du Livre. Paris).
Mustard, Wilfred P.
  "E. K's Classical Allusions," M. L. N., XXXIV: 193–203.
Myers, Frederick W.
  Classical Essays (London, 1879).
Nadal, Thomas W.
  "Spenser's 'Muiopotmos' in relation to Chaucer's 'Book of the Duchess'," P. M. L. A., XXV: 640–57.
Nash, Thomas.
  The Works of Thomas Nash (ed. by R. B. McKerrow; London, 1904–1910).
Nettleship, Henry.
  Essay on the Poetry of Virgil in connection with his life and times (Oxford, 1879).
Nicholson, Joseph S.
  Life and Genius of Ariosto (London, 1914).
Nitchie, Elizabeth.
  Virgil and the English Poets (Columbia University Press, 1919).
Nolhac, Pierre.
  Pétrarque et l'humanisme (nouvelle édition remaniée et augmentée. Paris, 1907).
Petrarca, Francesco.
  De contemptu mundi, colloquiorum liber quem secretum suum inscripsit (Bernae, 1604).
  The Life of Solitude (translated by Jacob Zeitlin. University of Illinois Press, 1924).
Pienaar, W. J. B.
  "Spenser and Ian van der Noot," *English Studies*, VIII: 65–72.
Pirisi, A.
  La Teorica di Torquato Tasso (Sassari, 1911).
Pope, Emma F.
  "The Reflection of Renaissance Criticism in Edmund Spenser's Faerie Queene," P. M. L. A., XLI: 575–619.
Prescott, Henry W.
  The Development of Virgil's Art (University of Chicago Press, 1927).
Rajna, Pio.
  Fonti dell' "Orlando Furioso". (ed. 2; Firenze, 1900).
Razzoli, Giulio.
  Per le fonti dell'Orlando Furioso (Firenze, 1900).
Reissert, Oliver.
  "Bemerkungen über Spenser's Shepheardes Calender und die frühere Bukolik," *Anglia*, IX: 205–24.

RENWICK, W. L.
"The Critical Origins of Spenser's Diction," M. L. R., XVII: 1–16.
Edmund Spenser, an Essay on Renaissance Poetry (London, 1925).

RIEDNER, W. L.
Spenser's Belesenheit (Münchener Beitrage, XXXVIII).

RONSARD, PIERRE DE.
Oeuvres complètes (ed. by Paul Laumonier; Paris, 1914–1919).
Oeuvres complètes (ed. by Prosper Blanchemain; Paris, 1857–67).

ROWE, FLORENCE E.
"Spenser's Shorter Similes," M. L. N., XIV: 32–47.

SAINITI, AUGUSTO.
Jacopo Sannazaro e Joachim du Bellay (Pisa, 1915).

SAINTE-BEUVE, AUGUSTIN.
Etude sur Virgile (Paris, 1891).

SANNAZARO, JACOPO.
Arcadia (ed. by M. Scherillo. Torino, 1888).
Opera (ed. by G. Bartoli. Venetia, 1741).

SAWTELLE, ALICE E.
The Sources of Spenser's Classical Mythology (New York, 1896).

SCALIGER, JULIUS CAESAR.
Poetices. Libri septem (editio quarta; in Bibliopolio Commeliano. 1607).

SELLAR, WILLIAM Y.
Virgil in Roman Poets of the Augustan Age, Oxford, 1883).

SHOREY, PAUL.
"Literature and Modern Life," The Atlantic Monthly, 141: 609–22.

SIDNEY, SIR PHILIP.
Complete Poems (ed. by Grosart; London, 1872).

SMITH, GREGORY.
Elizabethan Critical Essays (Oxford, 1904).

SPENSER, EDMUND.
Complete Poetical Works (Cambridge edition, 1908).
The Faerie Queene (ed. by John Upton; London, 1785).
The Faerie Queene, Book V (ed. by Alfred B. Gough. Oxford, 1918).
The Shepheardes Calendar (ed. by C. H. Herford. London, 1914).

SPERONI, SPERONE.
Dialoghi del Sig. Speron Speroni, di nuovo ricorretti (Venetia, MDXCVI).

STANYHURST, RICHARD.
Preface to the Aeneid in Elizabethan Critical Essays, I: 135–47.

STORER, WALTER H.
Virgil and Ronsard (Paris, 1923).

SYMONDS, JOHN ADDINGTON.
The Renaissance in Italy (New York, 1887).

Tasso, Torquato.
  La Gerusalemme liberata (ed. by A. Soleriti. Firenze, 1885).
  Il Goffredo overo La Gerusalemme liberata, col commento del Beni (Padoua, 1616).
  Discorsi del Signor Torquato Tasso dell'arte poetica: et in particolare del Poema Heroico, et insieme il primo libro delle lettere (Venetia, 1587).
Terzaghi, Nicola.
  L'Allegoria nelle Egloghe di Virgilio (Firenze, 1902).
Theocritus.
  The Idylls and Epigrams (ed. 5; ed. by Herbert Kynaston. Oxford, 1892).
Thompson, Guy Andrew.
  Elizabethan Criticism of Poetry (Menasha, Wisconsin, 1914).
Upton, Alfred.
  The French Influence on English Literature (Columbia University Press, 1911).
Vauquelin de la Fresnaye.
  Diverses Poésies (ed. by M. J. Travers. Paris, 1869).
Publius Virgilius Maro.
  Opera: ex recensione J. Conington (Novi Eboraci, MDCCCLXXX).
  Ciris epyllion pseudovergilianum (ed. by Geyza Nemethy. Budapest, 1909).
  Le Culex; Poème pseudo-Virgilien (ed. by C. Plésent. Paris, 1910).
  Appendix Virgiliana (ed. by R. Ellis. Oxford, 1907).
Vida, Marco Girolamo.
  De Arte Poetica (Tr. by Christopher Pitt in English Translations from Ancient and Modern Poems, by various authors, London, 1810).
Vivaldi, Vincenzo.
  La Gerusalemme Liberata studiata nelle sue fonti (Trañi, 1901).
Warton, Thomas.
  Observations on the Fairy Queen of Spenser (a new edition. London, 1807).
Willcock, Gladys D.
  "A Hitherto Uncollated Version of Surrey's Translation of the Fourth Book of the 'Aeneid'," M. L. R., XVII: 131-49.
Winbolt, S. E.
  Spenser and his Poetry (London, 1912).

INDEX OF NAMES

Achilles, 366.
Aeneas, 293, 329–38, 346, 354–6, 359–62, 367, 369, 371, 374–7, 391, 394, 401–5.
Aeneas Sylvius, 400.
Aeolus, 402.
Aesculapius, 372.
Alamanni, Luigi, 300.
Alcibiades, 290–1.
Alcina, 359, 368.
Aldus, 392.
Alençon, Duc de, 359, 364.
Alexander, 380.
Alidine, 392.
Amadis, 322.
Amathusia, 351.
Anchises, 334–6, 342, 355, 367, 390, 402.
Andromache, 303.
Angelica, 361.
Antiochus, 380.
Apollo, 403.
Apollonius of Rhodes, 354, 398 n.
Arcas, 346.
Argante, 324 n.
Ariosto, 322–5, 354, 357, 359, 361, 368–9, 372, 385–6, 394.
Aristaeus, 370–1.
Aristotle, 324, 405.
Artegal, 348, 355, 366, 384.
Arthur, 329, 330, 332, 338, 365–6, 391.
Ascanius, 303.
Ascham, 385.
Assaracus, 338–9.
Astolpho, 368, 372.
Ate, 379, 380.
Astraea, 363.
Astyanax, 303.
Augé-Chiquet, Mathieu, 269, 270, 272, 395.

Augustine, Saint, 362 n, 400, 406.
Augustus, 287 n, 292, 304, 312, 320–1, 339.
Azzolino, Alberico di, 323, 346.
Bacon, Francis, 327.
Baif, Jean Antoine de, 265, 269–80, 283–5, 288, 300, 305, 308, 353 n, 372 n, 395.
Baskerville, C. R., 398.
Beatrice, 362–3, 405.
Bellay, Joachin du, 265–8, 285, 305–6, 327, 340–2, 386.
Belleau, Remi, 269.
Belphoebe, 358–64.
Bembo, Pietro, 313–4.
Beni, Paolo, 325.
Bentley, Richard, 346 n.
Bernard of Chartres, 401.
Berni, Francesco, 322, 346.
Biblis, 351.
Bion, 271, 302.
Blanchard, H. H., 324 n.
Blanchemain, P., 288 n.
Boccaccio, Giovanni, 266–8, 279 n, 288, 301, 317, 340, 369.
Boethius, 362 n.
La Boëtie, Hector, 289.
Boiardo, Matteo, 322–4, 325 n, 357.
Bradamante, 348, 354–5, 357.
Braggadocchio, 359, 364.
Bridges, Robert, 376.
Britomart, 333, 338, 348, 350, 353–5, 357–8, 365.
Britomartis, 354.
Brunetière, Ferdinand, 266, 326.
Brutus, 336–9, 365.
Burton, Robert, 291, 321.
Bussi, Giovanni Andrea, 312.
Byron, G. G., 399.
Cador, 366.

Caesar, J. C., 345.
Calidore, 366.
Camden, William, 329, 330, 345, 365.
Camilla, 357-9.
Camoens, Luiz de, 319.
Carew, Richard, 321.
Carme, 348, 354.
Castiglione, Baldassare, 340, 388-9.
Caxton, William, 337.
Cazamian, Louis, 347.
Celaeno, 378-9.
Cellini, Benvenuto, 326.
Chamard, Henri, 267, 327, 341-2, 345, 397 n.
Chapman, George, 326-7, 389.
Charlemagne, 322.
Chateaubriand, F.-R. de, 342.
Chaucer, Geoffrey, 268, 271 n, 305, 308, 321, 336, 380.
Cheke, John, 385.
Cicero, 346.
Cinthio, Giraldi, 324, 355.
Circe, 303.
Cola di Rienzi, 292.
Colin Clout, 268, 319.
Cory, H. E., 271 n.
Contemplation, 402.
Cowley, Abraham, 382.
Crane, C. W., 361.
Crittenden, A. R., 384-5.
Croce, Benedetto, 385.
Croesus, 380.
Cupid, 387.
Danaids, 375.
Daniel, Samuel, 347.
Dante, 268, 308, 311, 323, 357, 362, 376, 401, 405.
Daurat, Jean, 265.
Deiphebus, 339.
Demosthenes, 346.
Diana, 293, 358, 361, 364, 387.
Dido, 335-7, 361.
Dis, 403.
Dodge, R. W. N., 354, 359, 394.

Donatus, 290 n.
Douglas, Gavin, 401.
Draper, J. W., 322, 324-5, 329.
Dryden, John, 307, 321, 382-4, 390, 400.
Dryope, 367.
Duessa, 309, 372, 381.
Edwards, E. W., 357.
"E. K.," 268, 271-2, 278, 287, 290-1, 293-4, 296, 302-3, 307-8, 317, 319.
Elizabeth, 292-4, 304, 359, 363-4, 398.
Emerson, O. F., 313-4.
Emerson, R. W., 328.
Ennius, 399.
Epidius, 292, 312.
Euryalus, 323.
Evander, 371, 392.
Ficino, Marsilio, 362.
Fletcher, J. B., 266 n, 268, 321 n.
Fletcher, Phineas, 319.
Frank, Tenney, 287 n, 311-2.
Frost, Robert, 308.
Fulgentius, 401.
Ganymede, 397-8.
Garsia, Augusto, 365.
Geoffrey of Monmouth, 337-8, 365.
Glaucé, 348, 353, 356.
Gloriana, 330.
Glover, T. R., 376, 398 n.
Goethe, 399.
Gonzaga, Scipio, 325.
Gorlios, 366.
Gough, A. B., 370.
Governar, 332.
Greene, Robert, 319.
Greenlaw, Edwin, 330, 332.
Greg, W. W., 296.
Grosart, A. B., 272 n, 289.
Guyle, 371.
Guyon, 330-2, 377, 387, 403-4.
Hall, Joseph, 285, 308.
Hardyng, John, 245 n.
Harper, C. A., 337.
Harington, Sir John, 299.

Harvey, Gabriel, 268, 288–9, 294, 296, 300 n, 304–5, 311, 325.
Hector, 366.
Heinze, Richard, 404.
Helen, 339.
Helenus, 355, 390.
Hellenore, 333, 339.
Herbert, George, 294.
Herford, C. H., 274–5, 296.
Hippolytus, 372.
Holinshed, R., 345, 365.
Homer, 304–5, 321, 325–7, 372, 382, 393, 400.
Horace, 397 n, 399.
Housman, A. E., 296.
Huizinga, J., 399.
Inachus, 338.
Iulus, 334–6.
Ixion, 373, 375.
Jebb, Sir Richard, 346 n.
Jeffrey, V. M., 340 n.
John of Salisbury, 401.
Jortin, John, 313–4.
Jove, 336, 372–3, 397, 404.
Juno, 359, 384.
Juvenal, 399.
Kerlin, R. T., 280 n.
Kitchin, George, 345 n.
Kluge, F., 320.
Koeppel, E., 325.
Lamartine, Alphonse de, 342.
Landini, Cristofero, 362, 402–6.
Lanson, Gustave, 265.
Latinus, 334.
Lavinia, 337.
Layamon, 337.
Lee, Sir Sidney, 346 n.
Legouis, E. H., 289, 347 n.
Leicester (Robert Dudley, Earl of), 292, 311–2, 314, 398.
Lentulus, 345.
Leonardo da Vinci, 327.
Lydgate, John, 268.
Lilly, M. L., 296 n.

Lodge, Thomas, 321.
Lorenzo de'Medici, 340.
Lowell, J. R., 398.
Lucan, 321.
Lucifera, 345, 380–1.
Mackail, J. W., 292, 327 n, 366, 376.
Machiavelli, Niccoló, 340.
Maecenas, 320.
Malbecco, 331.
Maleger, 393.
Malory, Sir Thomas, 322.
Mammon, 377.
Mandricardo, 366.
Mantuan, 267, 271 n, 279 n, 305, 317, 320.
Marcellus, 354.
Marfisa, 357.
Marie de Romieu, 269.
Marius, 345.
Marlowe, Christopher, 294.
Marot, Clément, 265, 267, 269, 271 n, 287, 301, 305, 317.
Mars, 387.
Matthew Paris, 337.
Maximus Tyrius, 290.
Medina, 330.
Medoro, 361.
Meliogras, 366.
Menendez y Pelayo, 300 n.
Mercilla, 364.
Merlin, 354–6.
Metabus, 359.
Milton, John, 303, 382.
Minos, 348.
Misenus, 367.
Montaigne, Michel de, 289, 392.
Moschus, 302.
Mustard, W. P., 302.
Myers, F. W., 357.
Myrrha, 351.
Nadal, T. W., 271 n.
Nash, Thomas, 304–5.
Nebuchadnezzar, 380.
Neoptolemus, 391.

Nettleship, Henry, 296.
Nicholson, J. S., 386.
Night, 309, 372–3, 381.
Nimrod, 380.
Ninus, 338.
Nisus, 323.
Nitchie, Elizabeth, 321–2, 401.
Nolhac, Pierre, 340 n.
Noot, Ian van der, 268, 329.
Oenone, 333.
Orpheus, 383.
Orsilochus, 358.
Ovid, 271, 323 n, 382, 384.
Palinurus, 367.
Pallas, 346, 392.
Palmer, the, in *F. Q.*, Book II, 354, 403.
Pan, 301.
Paridel, 331, 333, 336–7, 339.
Paris, 333.
Pasiphae, 351.
Peele, George, 340.
Peletier, Jaques, 300.
Penthesilea, 357–8.
Persius, 399.
Petrarch, 267–8, 292, 317, 340, 362 n, 402, 406.
Phaer, Thomas, 290 n, 385, 391–2.
Phantastes, 338.
Pienaar, W. J. B., 268, 329.
Plato, 290, 328.
Plésent, Charles, 312 n, 313.
Pluto, 372–3, 377.
Polydorus, 369.
Pompey, 345.
Pope, E. F., 306, 385 n.
Prescott, H. W., 287 n, 288, 404.
Priam, 333.
Puttenham, George, 306.
Pyrochles, 391.
Quirino, Girolamo, 313.
Radigund, 384.
Rajna, Pio, 322–3, 354, 369.
Raleigh, Sir Walter, 288, 364, 401.

Razzoli, Giulio, 357.
Redcross, 345, 357, 368, 402, 405.
Reissert, Oliver, 279 n, 380 n.
Renwick, W. L., 266 n, 290 n, 292, 300 n, 305–6, 385 n, 386.
Ricciardetto, 324 n.
Riedner, W. L., 301, 346 n, 392, 395.
Rogero, 348, 354, 368.
Romulus, 334–6, 345.
Ronsard, Pierre de, 265–9, 272, 278, 281–5, 287, 288 n, 296–9, 300, 305–7, 319, 326–30, 386–90.
Rousseau, J. J., 296.
Rowe, F. E., 393.
Rucellai, Bernardo, 340.
Rucellai, Giovanni, 300.
Ruddymane, 383.
Sainte-Beuve, Augustin, 318, 342.
Sainiti, Augusto, 340 n.
Sannazaro, Iacapo, 266–8, 270–2, 280, 296, 299, 317, 340–1.
Sansjoy, 372.
Satyrane, 324 n, 333.
Sawtelle, A. E., 339, 367, 372 n.
Scaliger, J. C., 312, 324, 326, 355, 389–90, 401–2, 404.
Scipio, 345.
Scylla, 348, 350, 358.
Sellar, W. Y., 298.
Servius, 287 n, 290 n.
Shakespeare, 289, 296.
Shorey, Paul, 401.
Sibyl, 354–6, 375–6, 387, 402, 406.
Sidney, Sir Philip, 272–8, 283–4, 303, 306, 308, 328, 400.
Sisyphus, 373, 375.
Skelton, John, 287.
Soardo, Battista, 306.
Socrates, 290–1.
Spenser, 266–9, 271–80, 282–5, 287–96, 298–309, 311–4, 317–26, 328–33, 335–40, 342–8, 350–4, 357–80, 382, 384–406.
Speroni, Sperone, 318, 405.

Stanyhurst, Richard, 399.
Statius, 379.
Storer, W. H., 272 n, 329 n, 386.
Stael, Mme. de, 342.
Strassino, 306.
Sulla, 345.
Surrey (Henry Howard, Earl of), 385.
Tacitus, 345 n.
Talus, 371.
Tantalus, 372–3, 375.
Tarchon, 324 n.
Tarquin the Proud, 345.
Tasso, Torquato, 322, 325, 362, 373, 382, 388, 390, 394, 405.
Terzaghi, Nicola, 287 n, 290 n.
Tethys, 367.
Theocritus, 266–7, 270–2, 274, 278, 280–2, 302, 306, 317, 353 n.
Theseus, 373, 375.
Thompson, G. A., 327 n.
Thoreau, H. D., 296.
Timias, 361–4.
Tisiphone, 375.
Tityrus, 268, 287.
Tityus, 310, 372–3, 375.
Trissino, Giangiorgio, 306, 324.
Tristram, 322, 366.
Trompart, 359–61, 364.
Turnus, 333, 337, 357, 361, 372 n, 391, 394.

Typhoeus, 373, 375.
Una, 405.
Upton, John, 324 n, 334, 355–6, 359, 361, 371, 384, 387, 391.
Uther, 338, 365.
Valerius Flaccus, 357.
Vauquelin de la Fresnaye, 269.
Venus, 293, 334, 336, 359–64, 387, 402, 405.
Vida, Marco Girolamo, 317.
Virgil, 266–74, 276–78, 280–5, 287–308, 311–14, 317–29, 331, 333–35, 340–2, 346–8, 354–7, 360–71, 375–80, 382–406.
Vives, Juan Luis, 287 n.
Volney, C. F. de C. de, 342.
Vulcan, 336.
Waller, Edmund, 382.
Walsingham, Sir Francis, 320.
Warton, Thomas, 295–6.
Webbe, William, 303–4, 391–2.
Whitman, Walt, 298.
Wilcock, G. D., 385.
Wilson, Sir Thomas, 385.
De Witt, Norman, 287 n, 292, 311.
Wordsworth, William, 296.
Wundt, W. M., 385.
Xenophon, 290.